On the
Line

Other books by Larry King

WHEN YOU'RE FROM BROOKLYN, EVERYTHING ELSE IS TOKYO

·

TELL ME MORE

·

MR. KING, YOU'RE HAVING A HEART ATTACK

·

TELL IT TO THE KING

·

LARRY KING

On the Line

The New Road to the White House

Larry King

with Mark Stencel

HARCOURT BRACE & COMPANY

New York   San Diego   London

Lyrics from "Don't Be Cruel (to a Heart That's True)" on page 35 copyright © 1956 by Unart Music Corporation and Elvis Presley Music, Inc.
Copyright renewed and assigned to Elvis Presley Music (administered by
R&H Music). International copyright secured. Used by permission. All
rights reserved

Library of Congress Cataloging-in-Publication Data
King, Larry, 1933 –
On the line: the new road to the White House/Larry King with
Mark Stencel.
p.   cm.
ISBN 0-15-177877-9
1. King, Larry, 1933 –   . 2. Presidents—United States—
Election—1992. I. Stencel, Mark. II. Title.
PN1991.4.K45A3   1993
324.973′0928—dc20   93-30892

Designed by Lisa Peters
Printed in the United States of America
First edition
A B C D E

*To CNN founder, Ted Turner, and CNN president, Tom Johnson,
whose foresight and vision made
all this possible.*

Contents

Acknowledgments

WRITING IS SUPPOSED to be a solitary act, but we have had enough people help us with this book to impress Cecil B. de Mille.

CNN president Tom Johnson made sure "Larry King Live" had the resources to bring you the campaign as we did—and bankrolled a lot of the fun documented herein. The commander in chief at the show during these events was Tammy Haddad, the most "effective maniac" to ever work in television. Executive Producer Tom Farmer has always been unflappable, level-headed, and a great source of Midol. Pat Piper, Mutual Radio's novelist-in-residence, also presided over a fair bit of election-year excitement. And thanks to Associate Producer Judy Thomas, my personal assistant, I didn't miss any of it.

Dave Berman, Duncan Campbell, Ashley Daniel, Korey Dorsey, Ellen Felvey, Julia Herz, Jerry Hollis, Kyle Kaino, Anne Powell, Carrie Stevenson, Katie Thomson, Booker Washington, Linda Wolf, and many others at the Cable News Network have forever changed the way presidential campaigns will be conducted and covered. And thanks to Alex Constantinople, our senior publicist at "Larry King Live," you know all about it.

We had two uncredited collaborators on this project. The prolific Larry J. Sabato, a professor of American government at the University of Virginia, offered up enough thoughts and ideas to write a book of his own on this topic. The bad jokes and any quotable quips are ours, but many of them were penned in his honor. Sandra Stencel, editor of Congressional Quarterly's *CQ Researcher,* generously donated her kitchen table and dining room as a work space. And, as Mark's devoted "edi-mother," she performed heroic acts in the preparation and polishing of this manuscript.

The real burden of editing, though, fell on Claire Wachtel at Harcourt Brace, and she came through for us time and again. Claire thinks she's a New Yorker, but she's really a Washingtonian. Please send all good political gossip her way. Harcourt's Leigh Haber was always tolerant and her guidance was invaluable. Ruth Greenstein patiently taught Mark everything he needed to know about publishing. We thank them for all their hard work on our behalf (and we can be pains). Proofreader Joe Sheehan saved us from ourselves (and does a great Tipper Gore impersonation). And thanks to Nicolle Nowitz for her persistent permissions work, constant message taking, and calming pep talks. (June lives.)

Daniel Herzfeld of the University of Virginia provided able research assistance, even if he writes for the wrong college newspaper.

Mark owes a special debt to Len Downie, Tom Wilkinson, and his many friends and mentors at the *Washington Post:* Chuck Babcock, Dan Balz, Bob Barnes, Steve Barr, Bill Casey, Karen DeYoung, E. J. Dionne, Tom Edsall, Bill Elsen, Ralph Gaillard, Megan Garvey, Ann Grimes, Jill Grisco, Bill Hamilton, Bob Kaiser, Howie Kurtz, Ruth Marcus, Buddy McAllister, Mary McGrory, John Mintz, Jo Rector, Jim Row, Barbara Saffir, Alan Shearer, Carol Van Horn, David Von Drehle, and Margot Williams. They and many others contributed to this story.

Fred Barbash, David Broder, Ann Devroy, Maralee Schwartz, and Bob Woodward have been especially supportive and encouraging. Heather Green, Lucy Shackelford, and Molli Yood are friends beyond measure.

Lucy White has straightened out sentences and suffered through more passages than any law student should be expected to endure. Eric and Kim, Chris, Wendy, Debban, Kelly, and Erika will be glad to have a friend back.

We must also thank the generous people at Mead Data Central, Inc., whose LEXIS and NEXIS services provided much of our research material.

Bob Woolf has made sure that I'll be around CNN long enough to do this again in 1996—and beyond. His daughter, our agent, Stacey Woolf, made it possible for us to tell you this story. Martin Lobel did his part, too.

Thank-yous to everyone who agreed to be interviewed for this book: Richard N. Bond, James Carville, Mario M. Cuomo, Michael K. Deaver, Phil Donahue, Marlin Fitzwater, Al Gore, Mandy Grunwald, Gary Hart, Sharon Holman, Tom Johnson, Brian Lamb, Ross Perot, Dan Quayle, Jack Reilly, Edward J. Rollins, Tim Russert, Bernard Shaw, Carole Simpson, Samuel K. Skinner, J. Dorrance Smith, John H. Sununu, Robert M. Teeter, Paul E. Tsongas, Margaret Tutwiler, and Jeff Zucker.

We also had lots of help from Lynn Appelbaum, John Bianchi, Karin Lippert, Eileen Murphy, Cathy Rehl, and Paul Sims.

Mark has extra thanks for his dear friends Lisa Dallos, Rayne Pollack, and Colette T. Rhoney.

And, as always, my love to Chaia King, Andy King, Herb Cohen and his wife, Ellen, and Martin Zeiger and his wife, Ellen.

To everyone who appeared on my show during the campaign, and everyone quoted in these pages, I am forever grateful, as I am to all the wonderful people I know in the great profession of broadcasting. We get paid to do this!

And thank you to the real talk-show revolutionaries—our callers.

In the end, a presidential election is like a traffic accident. Any two witnesses may see a completely different event. This is the way I saw the wreck. I wasn't in the car, but I had a good view from the corner.

By permission of Mike Luckovich and Creators Syndicate.

Chronology

During the 1992 campaign, television became an "electronic town hall," as Ross Perot often put it, with the presidential and vice presidential candidates answering the voters' questions directly on CNN's "Larry King Live" and other programs. Sometimes viewers phoned in their questions, sometimes the audiences were live. Here are some highlights from the "talk show" campaign:

DEC. 5, 1991: Two Democratic primary candidates, former California governor Edmund G. ("Jerry") Brown and former Massachusetts senator Paul E. Tsongas, answer audience and caller questions on "Donahue."

FEB. 14, 1992: Senator Tom Harkin of Iowa, a Democratic primary challenger, answers viewer calls on C-SPAN.

FEB. 17, 1992: Brown appears on a C-SPAN call-in show on the eve of the kick-off primary in New Hampshire.

FEB. 19, 1992: Conservative commentator Patrick J. Buchanan appears on CNN's "Larry King Live" to answer calls and discuss his surprising showing against President Bush in New Hampshire.

FEB. 20, 1992: Ross Perot, in his fourth appearance on "Larry King Live" in thirteen months, offers to run for president as an independent, if his supporters organize themselves and place his name on the ballot in fifty states.

FEB. 26, 1992: Harkin appears on "Larry King Live."

MARCH 23, 1992: Brown appears on "Donahue," the day before his upset victory over Governor Bill Clinton of Arkansas in the Connecticut primary.

MARCH 24, 1992: Perot appears on "Donahue" to answer audience and caller questions. MCI Communications Corporation reports eighteen thousand calls to Perot's toll-free line in thirty seconds when the phone number flashes on the screen at the end of the show.

MARCH 25, 1992: Brown takes calls on "Larry King Live."

MARCH 31, 1992: Retired admiral James Stockdale, Perot's running mate, appears on "Larry King Live."

APRIL 1, 1992: On "Donahue," Clinton answers persistent questions from his host about his personal life. Members of the audience criticize both Donahue and his questions, even booing him.

On "Larry King Live," Buchanan debates U.S. aid to Russia with Senator Richard Lugar, an Indiana Republican.

APRIL 2, 1992: Brown answers questions on "Donahue," his second appearance on the program in ten days.

APRIL 6, 1992: On "Donahue," Clinton and Brown "debate" without an audience or a host, asking each other questions for an hour on the eve of critical primaries in New York and two other states. Clinton wins in all states on April 7. Tsongas, who suspended his candidacy in March, beats Brown in New York but decides to remain on the sidelines.

APRIL 16, 1992: Perot appears on "Larry King Live" for the first time since unofficially announcing his candidacy on the show.

JUNE 2, 1992: Clinton, after practically securing his party's nomination with primary victories in California and other states, answers viewer phone calls on a CBS "town meeting" hosted by anchor Dan Rather.

JUNE 4, 1992: Clinton makes his first appearance on "Larry King Live" via satellite from Little Rock, Arkansas, the night after he played the saxophone on "The Arsenio Hall Show."

JUNE 9, 1992: Clinton takes calls on NBC's "Today."

JUNE 11, 1992: Perot answers viewer questions on "Today."

JUNE 15, 1992: On "CBS This Morning," Clinton answers questions from studio audiences in California, New York, Connecticut, Florida, Michigan, and Oklahoma.

JUNE 16, 1992: A live audience of young voters quizzes Clinton on MTV.

JUNE 18, 1992: Clinton answers callers' questions from Little Rock on "Larry King Live" for the second time in two weeks.

JUNE 24, 1992: Perot responds on "Larry King Live" to criticism by Republican and administration officials by accusing the GOP of engaging in "dirty tricks." Perot's remarks prompt a phone call from Republican party chairman Rich Bond who challenges him to substantiate his charges.

JUNE 29, 1992: On an ABC special hosted by anchor Peter Jennings, Perot answers questions from studio audiences in Arkansas, California, Florida, Iowa, Massachusetts, Michigan, Texas, Washington, and Washington, D.C.

JUNE 30, 1992: Clinton answers viewer phone calls on "Today."

JULY 1, 1992: Bush answers questions on "CBS This Morning" from a live audience in the Rose Garden at the White House.

JULY 15, 1992: Senator Al Gore of Tennessee, Clinton's running mate, appears (in suspenders with no jacket) on "Larry King Live" during the Democratic National Convention in New York.

JULY 17, 1992: Perot, appearing on "Larry King Live" in New York, explains his decision the previous day to withdraw from the presidential race. Angry and upset supporters, including Cher, phone in to urge him to reconsider.

JULY 22, 1992: Vice President Dan Quayle, answering a hypothetical question on "Larry King Live," makes headlines when he says that he would support his daughter if she decided to have an abortion.

AUG. 10, 1992: Clinton and Gore field questions from studio audiences in California, Colorado, Florida, New York, Ohio, Oregon, and Texas on "CBS This Morning."

SEPT. 9, 1992: Gore, on location in New Orleans, Louisiana, answers viewer phone calls on "Larry King Live," including an anonymous call from his wife, who asks him out on a date.

SEPT. 11, 1992: Non-candidate Perot takes calls on C-SPAN.

SEPT. 28, 1992: Three days before reentering the presidential race, Perot appears on "Larry King Live" on location in Dallas, Texas, where he is meeting with coordinators from his volunteer movement.

OCT. 4, 1992: Bush appears on "Larry King Live" in a recorded interview from the White House. The president promises to return to the show and answer viewer phone calls.

Perot appears on a C-SPAN call-in program.

OCT. 5, 1992: During one of their bus trips, Clinton and Gore appear on "Larry King Live" together on location in Ocala, Florida.

OCT. 6, 1992: Clinton and Gore appear together on "Donahue" from Nashville, Tennessee.

OCT. 7, 1992: On location in San Antonio, Bush answers viewer calls on "Larry King Live," his second appearance on the show that week. The president tells Clinton to "level with the American people" about his trip to Moscow and his participation in anti–Vietnam War protests while he was a Rhodes Scholar studying in England.

OCT. 15, 1992: In their second debate, Bush, Clinton, and Perot answer questions from moderator Carole Simpson of ABC News and more than two hundred undecided voters in Richmond, Virginia.

OCT. 21, 1992: Gore takes questions from a live audience of young voters on MTV.

OCT. 26, 1992: Clinton and Gore answer questions from a live audience in Winston-Salem, North Carolina, on "CBS This Morning."

OCT. 27, 1992: Quayle displays Perot-like charts while taking calls on "Larry King Live."

OCT. 28, 1992: Bush answers caller questions from Lima, Ohio, on ABC's "Good Morning America."

Clinton takes viewer questions on NBC's "Today."

Clinton also appears on "Larry King Live" from Louisville, Kentucky. He responds to Quayle's Perot-like charts from the previous night with Perot-like charts of his own.

OCT. 29, 1992: Perot appears on "Larry King Live" for the sixth time in 1992. (No charts.)

OCT. 30, 1992: Clinton fields questions from breakfasting patrons at a diner in East Rutherford, New Jersey, on ABC's "Good Morning America."

Gore answers viewer calls on C-SPAN.

Bush takes calls on "Larry King Live" in Racine, Wisconsin. Senior Clinton aide George Stephanopoulos phones in to challenge the president about his role in the Iran-Contra affair. Bush accuses Stephanopoulos of "desperation" politics.

NOV. 3, 1992: Clinton defeats Bush and Perot to become the forty-second president of the United States.

On the
Line

Signe Wilkinson, Cartoonists and Writers Syndicate.

Introduction

FOR TWO FULL HOURS the president sat in the Oval Office answering phoned-in questions from the public—from Mililani, Hawaii, to Brooklyn, New York. The dairy farmer's wife in Brandon, Wisconsin, wanted to discuss rural incomes and farm commodity prices. The thirteen-year-old from Ridgecrest, California, wondered if the government could transport snow from the East to his drought-struck state in freight trains. A recent college graduate from Rehoboth, Massachusetts, asked if the president had ever considered joining the astronauts on a space mission.

Of the nearly ten million people who tried to get through on a toll-free line that Saturday, forty-two callers from half the states in the Union reached the president with their questions. But it wasn't on my show. It wasn't on "Donahue" or "Nightline" or the "Today" show either. It wasn't even in 1992.

On March 5, 1977, President Jimmy Carter sat with CBS anchorman Walter Cronkite in front of his West Wing fireplace, fielding callers' questions for the CBS Radio Network. "This is a unique occasion, in the sense that it marks a new approach to communication between the president and the people of the United States," Cronkite said at the beginning of the live program, which was replayed later on public television. "It is indeed historic . . . and we must also say an experiment since the president has never taken part in this sort of broadcast."[1]

And that's the way it was, an experiment in democracy that remained in the test tube for another fifteen years. It wasn't until October 1992, when a struggling George Bush appeared on my show, that an incumbent president felt he should answer his constituents' questions on a national call-in show—no experts, no journalists, no hand-picked audiences—just the people and their leader. Welcome to the talk-show revolution, Mr. President.

In 1992 the public switched places with the campaign press. This time around, voters interviewed the candidates while the journalists watched. It happened on ABC's "Good Morning America," NBC's "Today" show, and "CBS This Morning"; on C-SPAN and on "Donahue"; on prime-time "town meetings" and on MTV. Even one of the presidential debates became a sort of talk show, with a live audience replacing the usual panel of reporters.

CNN's "Larry King Live," the international call-in show I'd hosted for more than seven years, seemed to be at the center of this talk-show phenomenon. The six major presidential and vice presidential candidates appeared on the show seventeen times during the election year, including ninety-minute interviews with each of the presidential contenders in the final days of the campaign. I asked all three—Bush, independent Ross Perot, and Democratic nominee Bill Clinton—if they would continue to appear on programs like ours if they won. All three said yes. "Absolutely . . . I'm going to keep doing them," Clinton said.[2]

Six months to the day after he took office, Clinton kept that promise, answering phoned-in questions in the library at the White House. And I was Walter Cronkite. Clinton answered questions on military base closings, a national lottery, taxes, and Bosnia. He seemed to be having a great time, and during a commercial break near the end of the hour, he offered to stay on the air with us for an additional thirty minutes to take more calls. As I explained to the president, the White House staff had said no when our producers asked them earlier in the day about extending the show.

"Do you think you and I can make this decision?" the president asked conspiratorially. "I'll take the blame."

When we came out of the break, I told the audience that we would be staying with Clinton a little longer than we had planned. "He would like to do it," I said. "We would be happy to accommodate."[3]

But Clinton and I did not know what had been going on offcamera in the White House. About twenty minutes into the show, Thomas F. ("Mack") McLarty, Clinton's chief of staff and a boyhood friend, received an urgent phone call. When McLarty got off the line, he huddled with other top White House aides, who then told our producers that they were considering pulling the president off the air at 9:30, half an hour early. Our producers talked them out of it, and they agreed to finish the hour.

The first commercial break after I announced that Clinton

wanted to stay even longer was a two-minute break ten minutes before the end of the hour. "I think we're going to have a problem," Tom Farmer, my executive producer, said in my earpiece. McLarty came into the library with senior adviser George Stephanopoulos, Communications Director Mark Gearan, and Press Secretary Dee Dee Myers. They did not want the president to stay on for the extra half hour. Clinton said it was too late, I had already told the viewers, but his advisers were insistent. Clinton asked if he could stay on for fifteen more minutes instead. When McLarty wavered, Stephanopoulos jumped in. "We're shutting you down at ten," the young adviser said gravely.

"Larry, please," McLarty whispered. "We'll owe you one."

I had no idea what was happening, but I knew we were running out of time in the break. "Go with them," Farmer told me. So I agreed.

The president looked as confused as I was. He thought the show had gone well, but now he wasn't sure. Had he said something wrong? "Do you think I'm going to fail?" he asked McLarty, as the chief of staff and the other advisers left the library. There wasn't time for them to answer.

There wasn't time for me to come up with an explanation for our viewers, either. "The president had another commitment he didn't know about, right?" I said, floundering a little. "There was another appointment which he was unaware of and we were unaware of."

The president nodded as I apologized and explained that he would join us again in another six months. "And I'll owe you a half an hour now," Clinton said.[4]

After we went off the air a few minutes later, the president invited me and some of our staff to the Lincoln Bedroom for coffee. McLarty said he needed to speak with Clinton first. "See you upstairs in ten minutes," Clinton said as the chief of staff led him to another room.

I asked Stephanopoulos what was happening. He said the coffee would have to wait until next time, too. U.S. Park Police had found the body of Deputy White House Counsel Vincent Foster, Jr., in a park near Washington, an apparent suicide. Foster grew up in Hope, Arkansas, with Clinton and McLarty. The president's advisers were afraid that CNN would break into the interview to announce the news or that someone would hear about Foster's death on a police scanner and call up to ask Clinton for his reaction. They did not want the president to find out on live television that one of his best friends had shot himself.

I could not blame Clinton aides for being nervous about that horrible possibility. Strange things—large and small—happen on our show. Clinton's attorney general, Janet Reno, had been scheduled to appear on April 19, 1993—the same day as the FBI's disastrous raid on a heavily armed cult, whose members had held off federal agents for fifty-one days near Waco, Texas. President Bush was our guest in late October, the same day new indictments in the Iran-Contra scandal raised old questions about his involvement in the controversial Reagan-era scheme. In February billionaire Perot scrambled election forecasts when he told our audience that he might be willing to run for president. Republican Party Chairman Rich Bond made news later in the year when he called Perot on the air to challenge his charges that the GOP was using dirty tricks against his campaign. When Perot temporarily withdrew from the race in July, Cher called, begging the independent candidate to reconsider. That same month Vice President Dan Quayle, a "pro-life" Republican, told our viewers he would support his daughter if she decided to have an abortion. The news gods seemed drawn to our program. Anything was possible.

What was it about "Larry King Live"? Why were political candidates so attracted to talk shows and call-in shows when those programs made them so vulnerable? There was no communications breakthrough. Carter and Cronkite had proved that a president could appear on a show like ours more than a decade and a half before. As for me, I was doing the same thing in 1992 that I'd done for more than three decades in broadcasting. I asked questions and let my viewers ask questions, like plenty of other talk-show hosts. So communications didn't change, and Phil Donahue and I didn't change, but the nation changed. Voters changed.

There was a revolution in 1992. It happened on shows like ours and it grew out of the public's distrust of, and disgust with, their poll-driven leaders—and their perceived coconspirators in the traditional press. The 1992 campaign marked an adjustment in America's low-calorie sound-bite diet. Deficits, taxes, recession, and scandal turned once-complacent voters—and nonvoters—angry with politics and the wasteful, inept government it produced. Moreover, the public saw the traditional press as snide, frenzy-driven trivializers who were contributing to the erosion of their democracy. Waning confidence in the media rivaled the public's anger at Washington.

Many in the fourth estate recognized that their vital role in the political process as analysts and truth squadders was in jeopardy. But as the campaign season got into full swing in early 1992, the top campaign issue—at least in the press—wasn't the economy,

health care, or the national debt. It was Clinton's marital problems
and draft record. Legitimate questions? You bet. The voters' number one concern? Hardly. But in February, when Clinton came in
second in New Hampshire's lead-off primary, the experts told us
he was finished. Two days later, after Perot unofficially launched
his campaign for the White House on our show, enthusiastic supporters jammed phone lines at his businesses. That was the start
of the real call-in campaign. Soon Clinton and, later, Bush would
follow Perot onto "Larry King Live" and shows like it.

The talk shows appealed to candidates because they could appear accessible, in touch with the everyday concerns of the callers
and viewers. For voters these call-in programs were a chance to
measure their would-be leaders for themselves, unfiltered. But many
in the conventional media were unenthusiastic about the influence
of the talk shows in the campaign, as they had been fifteen years
earlier, when Carter first tested the call-in format as a tool for
circumventing the press.

"Talk-show democracy" is certainly not without risks or flaws.
Our callers ask better, more serious questions than some in the
press give them credit for. But some candidates and their handlers
still think of talk shows as a way to avoid tough press grillings.
Talk shows should supplement the campaign press, not replace it.
There's room enough for everyone.

Our shows are also a good forum for exploring a candidate's
character. We can humanize candidates, draw them out, explore
their way of thinking—and expose their weaknesses. But in
humanizing our leaders, we may be helping to convert them
from statesmen into celebrities. It's only a matter of time before the supermarket tabloids give us Bill Clinton's ten-step plan

for trimming that waistline. That's when we'll know we've gone too far.

Campaign 1992 was a whirlwind. Sometimes my producers and staff and I felt a storm had swept us off to Oz. I remember watching a clip from a Clinton speech at Drew University in New Jersey on the news one night in late September. CNN had just announced Bush's first appearance on our show—a taped interview from the White House, with no viewer calls—and Clinton was challenging Bush to turn the show into a face-to-face debate. "What I think is Larry King ought to have us both on there and let the American people call in their questions," he said. "Then we get the best of all worlds—one moderator and millions of questioners."[5] I changed the channel, and there he was on another network—the presidential front-runner plugging our show. And the crowds were eating it up. Meanwhile the incumbent president was trying out his own town meeting format at "Ask George Bush" rallies arranged by his campaign. "Welcome to the Phil Donahue show," Bush told one such audience in Pennsylvania.[6]

The 1992 election spotlighted us like that, and it made me circumspect. Will talk shows' prominent role in politics outlive the voter anger of 1992? Should we do anything different in 1996? What sort of leaders will our format generate? Was the talk-show revolution a test run for the "electronic town hall" Ross Perot described so often during his campaign?

Those are some of the questions I've been asking as I reflect on that "wacky year," as Bush repeatedly put it. The ways "Larry King Live" and shows like it are changing the political process will have serious consequences for future campaigns and future governments.

That traditional journalists may scoff and turn up their noses will hardly surprise their critics.

That President George Bush and his campaign were so slow in discovering our revolution explains a lot about why they lost. But that's another story.

By permission of Mike Luckovich and Creators Syndicate.

"Beneath the Dignity of the White House"

THERE'S SOMETHING TIMELESS about Christmas parties at the White House. The Singing Sergeants' carols, the ornate traditional decorations, even the historic mansion itself fuse to create an illusion of permanence. It was December 1991, less than eleven months before George Bush's reelection defeat, but who could have known what sort of year it would be? It was an upbeat affair, and Bush and the First Lady were terrific hosts, as always, singing festive Christmas songs with their guests.

"I know my wish for 1992, Larry," the president said, greeting me in the receiving line. "What's yours?"

"Why don't you do the show?" I suggested.

"Nice try, Larry," Barbara Bush said. The line moved on.

It's hard to remember now what a safe bet Bush once was for

a second term, even as late as that Christmas. Recession had driven down the president's approval rating from its lofty peak the previous winter, immediately following the Gulf War, but no serious challenger had emerged. In New Hampshire, the site of February's lead-off primary, a handful of little-known Democrats were sparring from town meeting to town meeting. Billionaire Ross Perot was just an outspoken and eccentric Texan; "Gennifer" was just "Jennifer" misspelled; and the economy was about to pick up.

My wishes for 1992? I wanted to interview the president, I wanted to see an exciting election, and I wanted the Orioles to go to the World Series. But none of them seemed very likely then.

By the following October Bush was trailing his Democratic opponent in public opinion polls, and I was back in the White House. This time, however, I brought a CNN crew to interview the president and Mrs. Bush for a special Sunday-night edition of "Larry King Live." We set up in the East Sitting Room on the second floor, between the Lincoln Bedroom and the entrance to the president's private quarters. We taped the interview early in the evening to play later that night, so we could not have our usual phoned-in questions from viewers, which was how Bush and his advisers wanted it. For most of the campaign the Bush team had resisted talk-show appearances, especially call-in shows like ours. So we were happy to finally have him on the show, but I made him promise to come back and face our viewers, as his opponents—and even his own vice president, Dan Quayle—had done many times.

"I hope you understand that we've just resisted call-ins in the White House," Bush apologized during the show. "Maybe I'm overly respectful of the trust that Barbara and I have to keep this place as dignified as possible. . . . But I look forward to coming on your show and answering any questions they can throw—curve balls, straight balls, fast balls."

"In baseball parlance," I told the audience, "he'll take 'em any way you can throw 'em."

"Well," the former Yale first baseman said nervously, "I'd like to get a few with the seam showing."[1]

Bush's reluctance to use the talk shows made no sense to me, especially when his rivals were clobbering him so skillfully on those very programs. Maybe I was biased, but call-in shows seemed like the perfect weapon for an incumbent who was struggling against the public's perception that he was out of touch. Maybe he *was* out of touch, and that's why it took him and his handlers so long to recognize that the call-in craze wasn't a campaign gimmick but a televised revolt. I don't know how quickly it dawned on me, but at some point I became "the master of ceremonies of the 1992 campaign," as George Will put it in a column a few weeks before the election.[2]

The day after I interviewed the Bushes in the White House, I was in Port Huron, Michigan, to deliver a luncheon speech. From there I was heading to Ocala, Florida, to interview Governor Bill Clinton of Arkansas, the Democratic nominee, and his running mate, Senator Al Gore of Tennessee. Unfortunately there were no commercial flights from Port Huron directly to Ocala. Not even USAir had come up with that route. So my Michigan hosts had hired a private jet to fly me from Washington to Michigan to Florida. A private jet. Not bad. But Tammy Haddad, my senior producer at CNN—and long-time protector—was mortified. The CBS news magazine "60 Minutes" was working on a profile of me then, and Tammy was concerned that CBS would film me jet-setting lavishly from speaking gig to interview in a private plane. "Remember," she told me over and over, "it's not your plane." The CBS crew met me at the airport in Washington, and, as always, I stuck close to Tammy's script. "It's not my plane," I was explaining as a uniformed man appeared to tell us to board the jet.

"Mr. King," he said, "your plane is ready."

During the Port Huron speech, a woman in the audience had asked how the campaign was affecting my daily life. I looked out at her and the crowd that had come to hear me speak, and the CBS crew that had flown with me on a private jet to tape them watching me, and the whole scene seemed to answer her question. Here I was, a guy from Brooklyn, being flown around to give speeches and talk to presidential candidates. (Ross Perot had told me he doesn't think I should get paid the nights I interview "all these movie stars."[3] Sometimes, Ross, I can't believe I get paid to do *any* of the things I do.)

After the speech I got an urgent message from my assistant in Washington. The White House was looking for me: Call "Operator One."

The First Operator patched me through to James A. Baker III. Baker had run Bush's presidential campaign in 1988 and was the president's most trusted adviser. He had resigned, somewhat unwillingly, as secretary of state in August to come to the White House to serve as chief of staff—and to rescue the president's floundering campaign. I'd only met Baker once, at a state dinner. Hello, good-bye. This time, on the phone, he thanked me for getting Bush to say on the air the night before that he could return to the State Department after the election. He was clearly pleased with the president's performance.

"That was a terrific show last night," Baker said. "When can the president come on again and take calls?"

Boy, had things changed! Like almost every other news organization and talk show, we had called the media affairs office at the Bush White House once a week for three years to invite the president on. We had little hope and no success. And now they were calling us.

Had the campaign affected my daily life? You bet. But the jet, the increasingly lucrative speeches, the interviews, and even Baker's call didn't seem as strange as they might have in 1991 at Bush's Christmas party, when I wondered if we would ever land the president as a guest. I thought Bush had made his true feelings about shows like ours clear in late June, in a speech at a Republican fund-raising dinner in Detroit. In his remarks then Bush complained about "all the noise from Politics '92: endless polls, weird talk shows, crazy groups every Sunday telling you what you think."[4]

I asked Bush what he meant by "weird talk shows" during a late-October interview—our third with him that month and the second in which he would answer viewer questions.

"Oh, Larry," Bush said. "Don't be defensive."[5]

I try not to be. I try to keep criticism in perspective. We in the "infotainment" business have gotten used to pious put-downs, especially from our peers in the traditional press. Many of the same campaign reporters who brought us Donna Rice and Gennifer Flowers, who spent more time studying Bill Clinton's draft record than his economic plan, who generated story after story about Bush's unfamiliarity with grocery store checkout scanners, Hillary

Rodham Clinton's cookie-baking abilities, and Dan Quayle's spelling, complained that talk shows were too "soft" to play such an important role in the political process. How could we compete?

Phil Donahue had faced this sort of condescension in past elections. Losing Democratic nominees Walter F. Mondale (1984) and Michael S. Dukakis (1988) both turned down invitations to appear on "Donahue," even though they were struggling in the polls. "While it is true our program has always suffered from the daytime tabloid, we're-not-quite-the-news attitude," Donahue says, "I thought, this is an awful lot of pretense to be summoning to deny yourself this free TV time."[6]

In December 1991, as another campaign was getting under way, Donahue hosted two Democratic primary candidates, former Massachusetts senator Paul E. Tsongas and former California governor Edmund G. ("Jerry") Brown, Jr.[7] No votes had been cast, but the press had already written off both men's candidacies. Off the air, Tsongas asked why their opponents hadn't come, too. Donahue said that the other candidates didn't think appearing on his show was dignified.[8]

That was "the wisdom of 1984 and 1988," Donahue recalls. "It's not presidential. You do not put your candidate on a stage that has featured male strippers. You just don't."[9]

I know how Donahue feels. We haven't hosted male strippers, but until recently even some of our colleagues at CNN thought of "Larry King Live" as a fluffy show-business show. In their minds we interviewed the stars, the authors, and the actors. We were the network's top-rated program and may have helped pay the rent, but the news operation thought the serious stuff was their domain. I didn't entirely disagree. I have often compared our show with the Style section in my local newspaper, the *Washington Post*. The news departments at the *Post* may help set the agenda in newsrooms around the country, but many Washington-area readers turn first to Style's gossipy features for the really entertaining stuff. Sometimes there's news in the Style section, but it's mostly for fun, and that's what I thought our show should be.

This way of thinking about our show began to change, especially within CNN, during the 1991 war in the Persian Gulf. In forty-three days a U.S.-led military coalition drove Iraqi occupying forces from Kuwait. And for forty-three days people all over the world were glued to their television sets. If Vietnam was the first made-for-television war, the Gulf War was the first cable-ready war. Satellite technology brought each air raid over Baghdad, each Scud missile attack on Riyadh, each briefing and press conference into our living rooms as they were happening. And as the first twenty-four-hour-a-day news network, CNN was better prepared for the laser-fast developments in the Middle East than were the news divisions at the pared-down broadcast networks.

CNN's ratings soared, and as the network's top-rated show, ours zoomed up, too. It would have been inappropriate—and probably bad for ratings—to cut from Peter Arnett's live reports in Baghdad to me asking some actor about his or her latest film. So, for the first time, we became a part of the mix in the newsroom. We interviewed the same newsmakers and experts our news staff was interviewing. We even had extended conversations with Arnett and other CNN correspondents in the field about the latest developments in the war. And our interactive format meant viewers could respond to and talk about the emotional images and stories we were sharing with them. Certainly no other network was doing that.

As we learned later, policymakers in Washington—and around

the world—tuned in to gauge public support for the war as it was being waged. During an interview later in the year, Vice President Dan Quayle told me that the president had used our show as a "barometer" to see "how the public was responding. . . . [H]e was going to do what was right, but once he decided what was right, he knew he had to bring along the public. . . . So with you, of course, and especially the interaction you had with your callers, it was very helpful to say, 'You know what they're saying on the Larry King show?' "[10]

I hoped the attention we received during the Gulf War would help us land an interview with candidate Bush during the following year's campaign. As it turned out, I was right—eventually—because the Gulf War led to Ross Perot's first appearance on our show, and it was Perot who ultimately legitimized the talk shows as campaign vehicles.

J. Dorrance Smith, a top TV producer who left ABC's "Nightline" to run the media affairs office in Bush's White House, says Perot's mastery of the talk-show format—and, more importantly, the way he used it to launch a national campaign—made it "necessary or incumbent upon the rest of us to enter into that format."[11] Or, as Clinton campaign strategist James Carville puts it, Perot made shows like ours "a part of the expected way to campaign."[12]

Perot was a candid, patriotic Texas entrepreneur and Naval Academy graduate who had devoted much of his life and riches to helping U.S. veterans and their families. In 1969, at the request of the Nixon administration, he funded his own unsuccessful effort to deliver Christmas presents to U.S. prisoners of war in Vietnam.

But he was best known for hiring a commando to train a team of his employees to save two coworkers from a prison in revolutionary Iran. It was a daring rescue, dramatically chronicled in Ken Follett's best-selling book *On Wings of Eagles*. Later the tale became a television movie, with Richard Crenna as the heroic businessman. In the mid-1980s, Perot made headlines once again as he did public battle with General Motors, whose board he'd joined after the automaker bought his Dallas-based computer company. Perot was openly critical of GM, whose business practices he said were archaic. His fellow directors eventually bought out his stake in the company.[13]

Perot's personality was as made for television as his life. He appeared frequently on ABC's "Nightline," the network morning shows, and other programs to address a wide variety of issues, from hostage crises to international trade and the national debt. And C-SPAN began airing some of his speeches, too. In fact, watching early Perot speeches and interviews was a lot like watching him campaign in 1992. He even used many of the same lines. In his campaign, for example, he would often accuse politicans of ignoring the national debt, like "a crazy aunt in the basement." In a speech in Washington four years earlier, just two weeks after George Bush was elected president, Perot had used that same analogy to explain the nation's brewing economic problems. "All the neighbors knew she was there," he said then, "but we never talked about it, right? And now we're saying, 'Let's do something. She's going to get out and kill a neighbor.' "[14]

Perot was as funny and provocative then as he would be as a candidate in 1992, but he wasn't talking about running for president yet. ("There's only one compelling reason to have me run for president," he quipped, when asked then why he hadn't run. "I can solve the immigration problem. We'd have everybody [in the United States] fleeing for Mexico in just three months."[15]) Nevertheless, viewers reacted enthusiastically to each appearance. "Every single time [Perot was on], people called, people reacted," says Brian Lamb, C-SPAN's chief executive officer. "When there was an opportunity to buy transcripts . . . they bought more than they bought for anybody else."[16] Whether he intended to or not, Perot was cultivating a national following.

After many requests Perot finally agreed to appear on our show on January 11, 1991, just days before U.S. and coalition forces in the Persian Gulf launched Operation Desert Storm. We were broadcasting from Los Angeles that week, and he had flown in from Dallas on his own plane to join us. It was the eve of the congressional vote authorizing the president to use force if Iraqi troops did not withdraw from Kuwait by January 15. Perot had already argued on "Donahue" against going to war with Iraq. And before we went on the air, this crew-cut antiwar crusader was on the phone, lobbying members of Congress in his brisk Texas twang to vote against the use of force.

"I think it is fundamentally important that the people understand all the nuances of this situation and that we not reduce it mindlessly to Super Bowl II," he told our viewers. "On January the sixteenth, when we see our people dying, we react in horror, we withdraw all support from our military forces and leave them hanging out there like we did in Vietnam. Now that's what drives me. First commit the nation, then commit the troops."

Perot blamed the Bush administration for allowing Saddam Hussein's forces to enter Kuwait to begin with and for helping build up the Iraqi military machine. "Why are we here?" he said. "We're here because we created a monster and now we don't like him. Well, what are our problems? He's got a nuclear capability. Well, let's look ourselves in the eye and say we helped him get it. He's got a chemical capability. Well, we helped him get that. He has a bacteriological capability. We helped him get that."

This was tough stuff from a man widely viewed as a fiercely patriotic conservative, whose advice—and money—had been valued by some of President Ronald Reagan's more adventuresome foreign policy and security advisers. Near the end of the broadcast, we received an angry phone call from Robert A. Mosbacher, then Bush's secretary of commerce. "Ross is an old friend," Mosbacher said on the air, "and I'm an admirer of yours. I'm disappointed, Ross. You used to tell me you should never talk about something you don't know anything about. . . . You know a lot about computers, but you can't possibly know what's going on over there like the people that are ready to fight and the president and the advisers and [Chairman of the Joint Chiefs of Staff] Colin Powell and all the other people around him."

It would not be the last time Perot would be accused of speaking out of ignorance, but he hardly seemed fazed by Mosbacher's attack. In August 1990, Perot explained, after Iraq had invaded Kuwait, Mosbacher's own department had "bent over backwards" to send a supercomputer to Iraq via Brazil. "Do you think that's in the national interest?" Perot asked the secretary.

"Ross, no more than when you agreed not to sell anything to compete with your former company, then you tried to get in and sell things to the state of Texas. So let's not get into personal views like that. . . ."

"Stay on the issues, guys," I said. This was great TV. We were running out of time, but Tammy told me through my earpiece that the network wanted me to keep them going.

"Bob, you're running, ducking, and hiding," Perot said.

"I have never run, ducked, or hid, and you know better than that."

"Okay, answer the question on the supercomputer. Why would we send them a supercomputer through an Iraqi front company in Brazil—and the State and Commerce Departments moving heaven and earth to do it—after we had troops in the desert? And finally Defense and CIA got it stopped. That was probably an honest mistake."[17]

And on and on. It was an astounding exchange. CNN kept us on the air for several minutes after the scheduled end of our show to let Perot and Mosbacher go at it. As C-SPAN and others had discovered, Perot was a lively performer. We had him on twice more that year. In the spring, after the Gulf War, he reflected on his opposition to the popular and seemingly successful operation. Some of the Democrats in Congress who had opposed the war may have been slinking quietly to the reviewing stands for parades welcoming home U.S. troops, but Perot stood his ground and continued to argue against the conflict. "There's no question in my mind [that] we could have resolved the whole thing without putting five hundred thousand men at risk in the desert," he said.[18]

Later in the year he came on the show to refute charges in Oliver L. North's autobiography. North said that Perot had offered to pay his legal expenses if the former marine and National Security Council staffer would fall on his sword for Reagan during the Iran-Contra controversy. Perot maintained that he had told his fellow Naval Academy graduate that North was honor-bound to tell the whole truth and promised to help if he would. Perot also produced a recording of the telephone conversation North had described in his book that seemed more consistent with Perot's version of the exchange.

"See, we have a world where everybody runs, ducks, and hides . . . ," Perot said, echoing his January exchange with Mosbacher. "I don't want to hurt anybody. I don't want to hurt Ollie North. On the other hand, I don't like for someone to turn something around a hundred and eighty degrees and lie about it."[19]

By the time we had Perot on for his fourth appearance, two days after the February 18 primaries in New Hampshire, the presidential race was in disarray. President Bush had enjoyed approval ratings in the 90 percent range after his victory in the Gulf. But in economically depressed New Hampshire, he faced stronger-than-expected opposition from conservative television commentator Patrick Buchanan, a former White House aide to Presidents Richard Nixon and Reagan and cohost of CNN's "Crossfire." Buchanan received 37.4 percent of the vote in the Republican primary, to Bush's 53 percent. (The rest went to others, including many write-in votes for Democrat Paul E. Tsongas.) It was the Jimmy Carter omen, the Gerald Ford omen. Could Bush be another one-term president? At least he had won more than 50 percent of the vote in New Hampshire—better than Carter or Ford had done. But no incumbent president had survived strong opposition from within his own party in the primaries to be reelected.

The only good news the Bush White House could find in New Hampshire came from the mangled and mangy lot of Democrats who had risen to challenge him in the fall. Clinton, once the media-declared front-runner, had been damaged by news reports about alleged extramarital affairs and suggestions that he had avoided the draft during the Vietnam War. The experts left him for dead, and Clinton lost in New Hampshire to Tsongas, who'd worked as a lawyer in nearby Boston since leaving the Senate in 1984. But Tsongas's monotone campaign for frugality and sacrifice was still being dismissed by most of the traditional press. The pundits said he was a boring candidate with strictly regional appeal. And no one was going to vote for another liberal Greek from Massachusetts, they said—especially one who had cancer.

Senator Tom Harkin of Iowa and Senator Bob Kerrey of Nebraska, on the other hand, entered the Democratic race in late 1991 amid some media hoopla, which placed them among Clinton's top-tier challengers. But neither senator connected with the surly voters in New Hampshire, and both of their candidacies soon collapsed under their own press-created heavyweight status. Jerry Brown, meanwhile, was beginning to generate some excitement with his campaign's oft-repeated toll-free telephone number, his one-hundred-dollar limit on campaign contributions, and his acidic anti-Washington message. But was America ready for "President Moonbeam"?

None of it seemed to make any sense, and no one seemed up to the job. Would Al Gore or Governor Mario M. Cuomo of New York ride into the race to save their party from certain defeat? And what would Bush do? Would he shed Quayle, whom some considered a vice presidential albatross, or even step down himself—as President Lyndon B. Johnson had done after his weak showing in New Hampshire twenty-four years earlier? These were serious questions in that strange February.

Public opinion polls showed widespread dissatisfaction with all the candidates from both parties, and there was plenty of speculation about what new candidacies might emerge. One name that kept coming up was that of Ross Perot, whose supporters were constantly encouraging him to run for president. Perot had always said no, but two weeks before his February 1992 appearance on our show, he hinted to a group of business leaders in Tennessee that he might be willing to run under certain circumstances. I'd heard about these remarks, so my first question for Perot on February 20 was very direct:

"Are you going to run?"

"No."

"Flat no?" I asked.

Perot seemed to have something to say. "We've got an hour tonight to talk about the real problems that face this nation and you, in effect, have sort of an electronic town hall. So I think we can serve the country by really getting down in the trenches, talking about what we have to do, and then doing it."

"Why not serve the country by running for its top office?" I asked.

The businessman explained that he could serve his country best in the private sector. "I feel very strongly that my contribution, if any, in this country is to create taxpayers, and I know we need more taxpayers," he said. "I would do anything I could to help this country because it's been so good to me. If I could come up [to Washington] for nothing and spend the rest of my life and contribute in a very tangible way, I'd do that in a minute. I owe this country that."

"But?"

"Getting all caught up in a political process that doesn't

work . . . ," he said, "I don't think would be—I wouldn't be temperamentally fit for it."

At this point I was beginning to feel a bit like Mark Antony, offering Caesar the crown three times. I gave up after a few more tries and then let Perot spend most of the rest of the hour wowing our audience with his Texas straight talk on national problems. Perot's solutions were not new. They were the same priorities he'd championed in speeches and in TV interviews for years: Creating an "electronic town hall" so voters could reclaim their rightful roles as the country's "owners," putting our "servants" in the government back in their place, driving foreign lobbyists into the sea, and, most importantly, balancing the federal budget.

"By the way," I said after a commercial break near the end of the hour, "is there any scenario in which you would run for president? Can you give me a scenario in which you'd say, Okay, I'm in?"

Perot's demeanor changed. He described how he'd been touched by all the "everyday folks" who had been writing to him encouraging him to run for president and how, if he were to run, he wouldn't want to fail them. "And so I simply would say to them and to all these folks who are constantly calling and writing, if you feel so strongly about this, number one, I will not run as either a Democrat or a Republican, because I will not sell out to anybody but to the American people. . . . Number two, if you're that serious—you the people are that serious—you register me in fifty states. And if you're not willing to organize and do that . . . then this was all just talk."

"Wait a minute . . . , " I said. "Hold it, hold it, hold it."

This was maddening. We only had a few minutes left in the show, and there were so many questions.

"Now stay with me, Larry," Perot said.

". . . Are you saying groups all across America—all across America—can now, in New York, Illinois, California, start forming independent groups to get you on the ballot as an independent, and you would then, if this occurred in fifty states with enough people, you'd throw [in] the hat?"

"I am not encouraging people to do this," Perot said.

But if they did?

"The push has to come from them," he said. "So, as Lech Walesa said, 'Words are plentiful, but deeds are precious.' And this is my way of saying, will you get in the ring? Will you put the gloves on? And do you care enough about this country to stay the course? Now I want you to promise also that, if we—," he laughed, "you know, got lucky and climbed the cliff, you wouldn't climb out of the ring the day after the election. You're going to have to stay there for the fight."

Perot was addressing the camera now, talking directly to the viewers. "Now recognize, you're listening to a guy that doesn't want to do this," he said. "I don't want some apparatus built. I don't want two or three guys with big money around trying to do it. If you want to register me in fifty states, number one, I'll promise you this: between now and the convention, we'll get both parties' heads straight. Number two, I think I can promise you're going to see a world-class candidate on each side. And, number three, by the convention, you might say, cripes, you know, it's all taken care of. But on the other hand, we're set, and if you're not happy with what you see, and you want me to do it, then I don't want any money from anybody but you, and I don't want anything but five bucks from you because I can certainly pay for my own campaign, no ifs, ands, and buts. But I want you to have skin in the game. I want you to be in the ring."

What a moment! Ross Perot, the Texas billionaire, had just told our viewers he was willing to run for president. Why? When had he decided? What changed his mind? Hadn't he just said he wasn't temperamentally suited for the job? Those questions would have to wait. We were nearly out of time. But I did have to ask one thing.

"Okay," I said. "We have to know something very important. . . . What does *H* stand for?"

"Henry," he said.

"We'll be right back with Henry, right after this."[20]

I was excited. I don't know if I recognized at that moment how significant Perot's promise to run was, but I knew there was a tremendous hunger for a new candidate—someone else, *anyone else*—to run. And I knew there was tremendous anger at Washington and its regular inhabitants. Perot seemed to have the power to tap into both pools of public frustration. But I didn't know if he could pull it off. What if he did? I felt like a cross between Dr. Frankenstein and a Hollywood talent scout.

In the days following Perot's appearance on our show, his enthusiasts jammed the phone lines at his businesses. Even unlisted numbers at his offices rang off the hook. After several days of gridlocked lines, Perot rented space near his North Dallas office and assigned a small team of employees to build a phone bank for his quickly growing army of supporters. Within a month he had a toll-free number, one hundred phones, and dozens of volunteers lined up waiting for a chance to man them.

Perot appeared on other programs, including "Donahue" and the network morning shows. He even answered viewer calls on NBC's "Today" show, as he had on ours. And viewers gobbled it all up. After his exciting appearance on our show, who knew what the guy would do? Would he formally declare? Would he drop out? Would he announce that he was really an alien being with telepathic powers?

"Are you prepared now," Donahue asked dramatically, "on the Donahue program, to tell these people who your candidate will be for vice president?"

Perot said he was not, "But I promise you this. . . ."

"What?" his discouraged questioner said. "You're going to go on Larry King and announce it?"[21]

Each TV appearance generated tens of thousands of calls to Perot's 800 number—including about eighteen thousand simultaneous calls counted by MCI the moment the number flashed across the screen at the end of Donahue's interview.[22] It was like offering free tickets to see the Beatles reunite as Frank Sinatra's back-up band. And, much to the delight of the rating counters at the networks, the viewership for Perot's appearances was unusually high, too. "There were really big numbers," says Jack Reilly, then executive producer at ABC's "Good Morning America."[23] Big ratings meant Perot could have as much air time as he could breathe on just about any show he wanted. And that much free TV was worth more to the billionaire's campaign than all the paid advertisements he could ever buy.

The significance of Perot's candidacy did not sink in immediately at the Bush White House. "Frankly," says Samuel K. Skinner, the former transportation secretary who preceded Baker as White House chief of staff, "we thought [Perot] was a little bit of an eccentric. And, to that degree, we didn't . . . take him quite as seriously as we probably should have."[24] By late spring, however, the Perot movement had grown to the point at which Bush and his advisers could no longer ignore it. His support in national polls was rivaling the president's—and eclipsing Clinton's—especially in Texas and California, key states for any candidate seeking an electoral majority. Newspapers were beginning to run stories about what would happen if no candidate won a majority in the electoral college. That raised the amazing Constitutional possibility that the Democratic Congress would decide who won the election. And reporters and voters were already asking congressmen if they would vote with their party or with their districts in that scenario. The once-undefeatable president seemed to be in serious jeopardy.

Not since Jimmy Carter warded off a rabid rabbit with a paddle[25] had a president faced such an unusual political challenge. But instead of challenging Perot on his own turf—on a talk show, perhaps?—Bush and his advisers chose to respond in as traditional a format as possible, a White House press conference. The message: Bush's long-standing support for a balanced-budget amendment, a proposal the president's advisers thought would let him address the Perotists' pet issue, the national debt, without having to address Perot. The reporters at this press conference had little interest in the balanced-budget amendment, but Bush skillfully found a way to slip the idea into nearly a dozen answers, no matter what he was asked. Would he debate Perot and Clinton in the fall? Did he think Perot was a man of principle? Was the public rejecting the president's message? It all came back to the nation's urgent need for a balanced-budget amendment—even when he was asked about abortion. "I am not persuaded that people all across this country vote on only one issue, abortion," Bush said. "I think they're interested in world peace. I think they're interested in education. I think they happen to be very supportive of a balanced-budget amendment."[26] Bush's performance was disciplined, but I doubt it inspired many Perot supporters to defect—even the ones who saw it.

The name of Bush's declared Democratic opponent hardly came up at the president's press conference, even though Clinton had just secured his party's nomination with a victory in California's primary. The Arkansas governor's approval rating was in tatters after the grueling Democratic nominating contest and its seemingly endless controversies. For months Clinton's campaign had spent most of its time putting out fires, answering questions about Clinton's marital life, his draft record, his college-age experimentation with marijuana, and so on. In the three-way race for president, battle-scarred Clinton was running a distant third. He even looked as if he might become 1992's William Howard Taft—the Republican nominee and incumbent president who came in third to Democrat Woodrow Wilson and third-party challenger Theodore Roosevelt in 1912. (Former president Roosevelt's 27.4 percent showing that year is still the highest ever for a minor-party or independent presidential candidate.)

Clinton's top strategists knew they had to do something even more radical than the Bush team to get the public to reexamine their candidate. So in April, following Clinton's win in the New York primary, these advisers launched what they called the "Manhattan Project," a massive research effort to figure out why their candidate was having such a hard time connecting with voters. Interestingly, these strategists discovered that Clinton was widely viewed as someone who'd been born with a silver spoon in his mouth. But the Manhattan Project research also showed that voters were willing to reexamine Clinton after they were exposed to details about his background and childhood: the poor boy from Hope, the father who had died before he was born, the abusive stepfather—all the born-in-a-log-cabin, George Washington-and-the-cherry-tree details that matter so much. The voters needed to hear some of the up-from-nothing stuff that had made Perot interesting before he'd ever said a word about the deficit. They had to know more about Bill Clinton as a person before they were willing to listen to the would-be president's ideas for the country. But how do you get them to pay attention to a guy who's running third?

The solution came from Mandy Grunwald, a young New York–raised TV junkie and Democratic media consultant. Grunwald suggested a "pop culture" campaign, one that would mean going around traditional news outlets, as Perot had done to cultivate his flock over the years. "The news covers new ideas, proposals, attacks," Grunwald says. "That's what makes news. That's what gets covered. . . . My recommendation was . . . [that] we had to go to nontraditional news sources because we were not trying to convey news. We were trying to convey biography and personality. You can't do that on the evening news."[27]

Grunwald's strategy grew out of the lessons learned in Clinton's primary campaign. That Clinton had even survived the primaries at all was a tribute to his gifts as a campaigner, especially in interactive formats. Clinton proved himself in that regard in town meetings all over the state of New Hampshire, where "retail" politics is so important that primary voters seem to make up their minds based on which candidate they've spent the most time with personally. So when the front-runner's support plummeted follow-ing questions about extramarital affairs and his draft record, Clin-ton's campaign bought two half-hour chunks on local television so he could spend some quality time with undecided voters, answer-ing questions from a live audience and viewers at home. These programs helped him win back enough support to place second in the Granite State. The Clinton campaign produced similar pseudo-talk shows of their own in several other tough primary states. Clin-ton also began using real talk shows, appearing twice on "Dona-hue," once on his own, and once with Jerry Brown.

Clinton's campaign devised a Perot-like plan for reintroducing their candidate to America that would rely on talk TV to showcase him in formats in which he could be seen answering the public's questions directly. At the same time he could avoid the "character questions" that seemed to preoccupy many journalists. This strat-egy produced a two-week interactive TV marathon in June. He joined CBS anchor Dan Rather for a prime-time town meeting and answered viewer questions during two call-in interviews on NBC's "Today" and one on "CBS This Morning." On June 16 Clinton sat for yet another question-and-answer session with a live audience of eighteen- to twenty-four-year-olds on MTV, the music video channel whose producers had launched a voter-education and registration drive they called "Chose or Lose." The Clinton campaign also bought time on NBC for a half-hour town meet-ing of their own. But, as Perot had discovered, there was so much free TV available they scrapped plans to buy more. "If the 'Today' show was willing to set up a two-hour town meeting, we thought, of course, let's do that," Grunwald says. "It's more credible, you get the same kind of questions, and we save money."[28]

Clinton also made his first appearances on "Larry King Live," on June 4 and 18, via satellite from Little Rock. The first show was on the same night as Bush's budget-balancing press conference. Unlike Bush, however, Clinton had no qualms about addressing their third-party rival. I asked him if he thought it was odd that he was hardly mentioned at the press conference, that Perot was the story.

"Well," Clinton said, "it may be odd. Folks like you have been pumping him up, with no program but with things that sound good. So it's just one of those things."[29]

I've come to be very impressed with Clinton, but I didn't warm to him as a guest right away. It is always harder to connect with a person who's hundreds of miles away than it is when they're sitting in your studio, eyeball to eyeball. But I also just wasn't much of a Clinton enthusiast at that point. In part I thought he deserved his "slick" reputation for evasiveness. And I'd been very offended by remarks he'd made about Mario Cuomo in a secretly taped exchange with Gennifer Flowers, the woman who claimed in January 1992 that she'd had a twelve-year affair with the Arkansas governor. Flowers said on the tape that she "wouldn't be surprised if [Cuomo] didn't have some mafioso major connections."

"Well," Clinton said, "he acts like one."[30] Clinton confirmed it was his voice on the tape and apologized for the remark. It still bugged me. Cuomo was a friend, first of all. But it was also a New York ethnic thing. As Cuomo put it at a news conference the day after Flowers released her tape, Clinton's mafia suggestion was part of the "ugly syndrome that strikes Italian Americans, Jewish people, Blacks, women, all different ethnic groups."[31]

Eventually, Cuomo was able to laugh Clinton's line off. He even nominated Clinton in a powerful speech at the Democratic National Convention in New York. "Now this is common knowledge," I said to Cuomo during an interview on the eve of the convention. "You're not crazy about Bill Clinton the person."

"Well, I'm not crazy about you, Larry, either," Cuomo said, laughing, "but I can work with you."[32]

I wonder if Clinton and I would have hit it off sooner had I offered him a chance to play his saxophone, as he did on late-night TV's "Arsenio Hall Show" the night before my first interview with him. That appearance on June 3 was probably the most sensational moment of Clinton's talk-show tour. He topped the program wearing dark Blues Brothers–style sunglasses, playing the show's theme and then Elvis Presley's "Heartbreak Hotel." Afterward Clinton and his wife, Hillary, sat for an interview with Hall, whom they handled deftly, with charm and humor, even when he prodded Clinton on his notorious ("I didn't inhale") marijuana explanation. "That's why I played saxophone," Clinton said. "That's how I learned to inhale. You die if you don't inhale."[33]

Clinton's Arsenio gig wasn't the first time he'd played Elvis impersonator during the campaign. In an interview before New York's primary in April, Charlie Rose asked Clinton if he would sing one of his musical hero's songs, as he reportedly did sometimes on the campaign plane. The ever-hoarse candidate happily obliged, thumping out his own beat with his hand on the table in front of him, singing:

> You know I can be found,
>   sitting home all alone.
> If you can't come around,
>   at least, please telephone.

"My message to the New York press:"

> Don't be cruel.[34]

The rendition got national air time on the "NBC Nightly News"—
and a smile from anchor Tom Brokaw. But it didn't generate anything like the criticism Clinton got for his "Arsenio" appearance.

"I don't know . . . ," said Cuomo, ordinarily an astute political observer. "You show me Bill—and I said this to his people—
with dark glasses, playing the saxophone, you know, and guys
like me would tell you, I don't think I would vote for [John] Belu-
shi . . . for president, may he rest in peace. But who knows? Maybe
there are people who like the Blues Brothers."[35]

The traditional press was even tougher. On ABC's "This Week
with David Brinkley," for instance, Tom Wicker of the *New York
Times* and Barbara Walters of "20/20" agreed that Clinton's performance had been unpresidential. "There's something about the
presidential candidate with his shades on, playing the saxophone
that's endearing on one hand, but not very dignified," Walters said.
Wicker pondered Clinton's "association with jazz music and dark
shades and Arsenio Hall"—and ended up sounding a lot like
the Church Lady on NBC's "Saturday Night Live": "When
two other candidates are making such a point of traditional
family values, whatever they are, for a guy to appear on television
playing jazz with dark shades on, on the 'Arsenio Hall Show' after
midnight, I don't think that enhances his standing on family
values."[36]

Even former Republican White House aide David Gergen, a
longtime Clinton friend and a respected pundit, was critical. "The
gap between Arsenio Hall and talking to someone like [British
Prime Minister] John Major to me is so dramatic, it suggests that
[Clinton] doesn't have a handle on what it takes to be president,"
he said on PBS.[37] (Gergen, by the way, left his job at *U.S. News*

& World Report in 1993 to serve as a senior adviser in the Clinton White House. Sorry, Arsenio.)

Grunwald had anticipated much of this criticism in an April memo to Clinton outlining her talk-show strategy. In this memo she warned her candidate that some of their plans might be dismissed as "unpresidential."

"Bullshit," Grunwald wrote simply.[38]

I have to agree. The "Arsenio" controversy was a classic example of dismissive Beltway dwellers laughing—even though the joke was really on them. The Democratic campaign's risky decision to do Hall's show helped them make Clinton look young and accessible. And it showed that he had enough of a sense of humor to laugh at himself. Pictures from the show appeared repeatedly throughout the campaign in print and on television, turning the scene into one of the election's defining images. It was a smart move. "We were trying to explain to people that this was a person," Grunwald says, "not a caricature like the cartoons in your newspaper, but a person who has a life. . . . I think explaining who you are is not unpresidential."[39]

Clinton's "Arsenio" appearance wasn't the first time a presidential candidate tried the razzmatazz route to the White House. Richard Nixon occasionally showed up on Jack Parr's late-night show, the first time during his 1960 race against John F. Kennedy. Eight years later, during his successful presidential bid, Nixon made a memorable cameo appearance on "Laugh In." "Sock it to me," Nixon had said stiffly.

In George Bush's stature-conscious White House, however, the wisdom of appearing on shows like "Arsenio Hall" was not apparent until much later. "My reaction was that [Clinton] made a mistake," recalls then – White House spokesman Marlin Fitzwater, "that it was a disaster, that people would not respect or vote for someone who trivialized himself by playing the saxophone and . . . bantering with Arsenio Hall. We were wrong."[40]

A few days later Fitzwater promised reporters that Bush would eventually make use of the same programs Clinton and Perot had been using to campaign against him. But the spokesman pointedly exempted "Arsenio Hall," provoking a memorable on-air tirade by the offended late-night host: "I remember being invited to the White House, and I declined the invitation," Hall told his nearly three million viewers in an opening monologue on June 10.

> But excuse me, George Herbert, irregular-heart-beating, read-my-line-lipping, slipping-in-the-polls, do-nothing, deficit-raising, make-less-money-than-Millie-the-White-House-Dog-last-year, Quayle-loving, sushi-puking Bush! I don't remember inviting your ass to my show. Tell him that, Fitzwater. . . . I don't need you on my show. As a matter of fact, my ratings are better than yours. Why do I need you? You're in trouble. Can you believe it? I'm a little guy from Cleveland. I got dissed by the president. At least I'm in good company, though. Now I've joined the ranks of the homeless, the unemployed, and the middle class. So I guess I don't feel so bad. I guess, Mr. Bush, he won't do my show, maybe he'll do "Donahue" when the topic is Relatives of People Involved in Savings and Loan Scandals. Maybe that's the show he'll be on.[41]

Bush never did that particular "Donahue" interview. In fact, it was a long time before he was willing to do any talk-show interviews at all. Why? Because the Bush campaign and White House were running on a "stature strategy," which is to say they were hardly running at all.

Early in the election process, Bush and his aides made a tactical decision to sit out the campaign, avoid partisan politics, and act "presidential" until August—after the Republican National Convention in Houston. Having Bush hawk himself on TV, like an actor plugging a new film or an author pitching a book, seemed inappropriate to the president. "He was often worried that if he went on one of these shows that we'd have the president talking about Desert Storm and cut away to a deodorant commercial," says John H. Sununu, Bush's first chief of staff in the White House.[42] Some of Bush's advisers still think they made the right decision. "I mean there's only one president, and he can't be on "Larry King" every week . . . ," says Skinner, Sununu's successor. "I think there's a risk of the president being overexposed and looking like he's too defensive. You ought to use this medium when it suits your needs, not just because it's there. And I think the president should use it sparingly."[43] Other Bush aides are less sure. "I think we virtually had lost the election before anybody realized the wisdom of doing these shows," Fitzwater says.[44]

There were other reasons why Bush and his advisers were uncomfortable with talk shows like ours. First off, Bush was a very private president. His New England modesty made him shift and squirm whenever the media tried to probe his inner workings. "I've found that in this line of work you always get psychoanalyzed," he once said, "and you're stretched out on a theoretical couch for people to figure out what makes you tick. That just goes with the job."[45]

Bush was right. That's exactly what people in my business do to people in his. I am an interviewer, not a journalist. I don't want to ask press-conference questions. I like to ask human questions, and I try to get human answers. That can lead to awkward, unexpected moments, of course. And sometimes those moments make news.

Vice President Quayle was a frequent guest on "Larry King Live." We were relaxed with each other on the air. He knew the kinds of questions I like to ask. When he came on the show in late July 1992, we got into a discussion about the issue of parental consent for teenagers seeking abortions. "My daughter, for example, if she wants to take an aspirin at school, she has to call and get permission," Quayle said. "If she wants to have an abortion, she doesn't. I'm not sure that's right. . . ."

"What if she did?" I asked. "What if your daughter grew up, had a problem, came to you with that problem all fathers fear? How would you deal with it?"

It seemed like an obvious question to me—a father who'd raised a daughter on my own from the time she was twelve. It was a deeply personal question, one that demanded a revealing answer, which may have been why Quayle looked so unhappy with the direction our conversation was going. But what could he say? No comment? He's a father. How can he have no comment on something like that?

"Well," he said, "it is a hypothetical situation . . ."

"Yes."

". . . and I hope that I never do have to deal with it . . ."

"I hope so, too."

". . . but, obviously, I would counsel her and talk to her and support her in whatever decision she'd make."

"And if that decision was abortion," I asked, father to father, "you'd support her as a parent?"

"I'd support my daughter," Quayle said. "I would hope that she wouldn't make that decision."[46]

Stop the presses! Had the conservative vice president in an antiabortion administration turned pro-choice? This question consumed a great deal of ink and air time in the weeks leading up to the Republican National Convention. It was asked in news stories and debated on op-ed pages. Politician Quayle's position on abortion had not changed, as the vice president, his wife, his staff and even the president explained—over and over again. But his comment was newsworthy because he had answered as a parent, not a politician. And Quayle's public and personal positions appeared to be at odds.

"I wasn't interested in making news there," Quayle says looking back. "I didn't think it was really that interesting, but the media did and they sort of jumped on this thing, and I really didn't want to make any news on abortion, period."[47]

Unfortunately for the vice president, the stir over his remark corresponded with reports about a "dump Quayle" effort within his party. Quayle weathered this frenzy as he had—and will—many others. But the controversy was an example of what made Bush wary about shows like ours. This was the danger for politicians who put themselves on the media couch. "President Bush personally was not comfortable with . . . personality-driven interviews," Fitzwater says. "He's always resisted them on a personal basis just because of who he is."[48]

Bush and his aides were also uncomfortable with the idea of his having to answer randomly phoned-in questions from the public. "It takes the middle man out, which I think can work to a candidate's advantage," says Smith, the media affairs director in Bush's White House. "The problem is that there's a lack of control. . . . [There was] great resistance to do anything that wasn't a hundred percent controlled."[49]

When reporters asked about the call-in phenomenon, Bush insisted that he liked audience-participation formats. He often compared what the other candidates were doing on TV talk shows to the voter questions he had answered during "Ask George Bush" campaign rallies ever since he first ran for president in 1980. In a June 1992 interview, for instance, CNN's Frank Sesno asked Bush if he'd "ever contemplated putting in an 800 number here at the White House or whether you intend to hit the talk-show circuit as your opponents are doing, taking calls from the viewers, having more of a dialogue?"

"I might give that a try," Bush said. "I like it. . . . I think it's good to take some questions and to be out there on the front line. But I think to turn the White House into a clearinghouse for 800 numbers is a little beneath the dignity of the White House, and I am determined to conduct myself in this office hopefully with decency and honor and dignity. So I am not going to do that and say, hey, call in to your friendly White House operator and use this magnificent building and this magnificent office I hold to further political ends in that way."[50]

The Rose Garden, however, was another matter. There, behind the West Wing two weeks later, Bush had his first nationally televised question-and-answer session with his constituents on "CBS This Morning." The president could no longer afford to keep the voters on hold. Perot had already topped Bush in some polls, Clinton was gaining ground—and both rivals' success was due in some part to their abilities as talk-show campaigners. "We were interested in . . . finding a format that allowed the president to be on the air longer than twenty seconds," Fitzwater says. "But [we wanted to] do it in a way that preserved the dignity of the office. And so doing it from the Rose Garden preserved a sense of dignity about it all and tended to take off the negative aspects that we saw from just exposing yourself in a form that could tend to trivialize the presidency."[51]

A live audience can only be so random. CBS pulled its 125 questioners from the White House tour line. But a fifth of them—even many children—were able to quiz the president for an hour and a half. The questions themselves were very much like the ones his opponents had already answered many times on other shows: What would he do to protect people's social security? What were his plans for speeding up the economic recovery? What was he going to do about gang violence, international trade, race relations, Cuba, the environment, health care, and so on?

I watched the CBS show at home and was struck by how nervous the audience looked, how deferential each questioner was. And I thought that was probably what the White House had wanted. That left cohosts Paula Zahn and Harry Smith to play media bullies. They followed up and pressed Bush on his political troubles, questions Bush insisted he wasn't ready to answer—yet.

"Why wait, though?" Zahn asked.

"Well, because I think it's prudent to try to do my job," Bush said. "We're talking here about issues that mean something to American families. . . . I'd rather concentrate on what I'm trying to do, or fail to do, than I would on some attack by somebody else. . . ."

"But if you don't set the record straight," Smith said, "you may not have that opportunity."

"Listen," Bush said, "I think people are tired of this long election series. It's gone on since before the first of the year. Day in, day out, some new poll, some new attack in a primary. I think people want to see the country move forward, get back to work, get educated. And so I think I'll reserve the definition of the others until . . . the campaign starts, which is later on. . . . I'm not dumb. I know we're in a campaign environment. But I'm not going to start attacking right now."[52]

Bush was still a reluctant talk-show candidate. As the polls got worse, however, he got better. In the last month of the campaign, he finally agreed to answer viewer phone calls, on our show and on ABC's "Good Morning America." He agreed to a ten-minute interview with an MTV correspondent in the final days of the campaign. However, he and his handlers rejected the music network's long-standing invitation to a face-to-face session with an audience of eighteen- to twenty-four-year-olds. "He just wouldn't do it, and part of that was generational," one Bush adviser says. "Even some of his children . . . really tried to talk him into it, and there was no way."

Clinton and Gore had accepted MTV's invitations and scored big points among its young viewers—a voting block that had voted Republican in 1980, '84 and '88. During one of the president's "Ask George Bush" events in late October, a young communications student at the University of Central Florida even asked Bush directly why he hadn't gone on MTV to try to reach more voters her age.

"I'm not too much of a mod MTV man," Bush said. "I can't play the saxophone, but I know a good deal about, you know, issues. And so you can't be everywhere." Anyone who'd ever paid much attention to the president's speeches could hear a Bushism trying to grind through the gears in his head. His aides must have been squirming. He rambled about trying to reach young voters with his proposals for health care, education reform, and student loans. "But look," he said, "there's something funny going on in American politics. . . . And I like it. I feel comfortable. But, you know, some of these programs, to get out there and kind of outdo Oprah or Phil Donahue, that's not my style. And maybe MTV would be a good one, and I'll think about it. But you can't do them all, and you shouldn't be judged by whether you go on one single network or one single program."[53]

"Nobody thought it was a good idea," Fitzwater says of MTV's offer. "It was an audience that we weren't going to win, that he wasn't familiar with. . . . [And] everybody had scary scenarios of [someone] asking him the top ten songs in the pop charts or something, and he couldn't name them."[54]

I suppose they had some basis for their fears. During a campaign swing in New Hampshire, Bush had repeatedly quoted a Nitty Gritty Dirt Band song he attributed to the "Nitty Gritty Great Bird." But the invitation from MTV seemed to me like another missed opportunity.

No single interview, or series of interviews for that matter, could have rescued Bush's campaign. The 1992 election, like most, was ultimately about the economy. But Bush could have used audience-participation programs—like ours, like MTV's—to appear sympathetic, to show that he understood people's problems, at a time when his opponents were using the accessibility that call-in shows create to make the president look "out of touch."

"It wasn't so much the shows, but the shows sent signals that reinforced what your enemy was saying about you," says Margaret Tutwiler, the former State Department spokeswoman who came with Baker to the White House in August. "I mean when you're in a campaign, people don't really care that you're president. . . . Yes, you fly on big huge airplanes—blue and white and [with] a big seal. But you are a candidate, there is an election, and people want to be asked for their vote. It's just the way it works." [55]

So should Bush have gotten into campaign mode sooner—hit his opponents, done the talk shows? During his third appearance on our show, four days before the election, an American woman living in Belgium phoned in and asked Bush that very question. "Some thought it was a little late," Bush said. "She may well have something."

"In retrospect, though," I asked, "might she be right? Might you have started sooner?"

"Well," Bush said, "I'll let her know on November fourth." [56] I wonder how he'd answer now.

Bush will be a great ex-president, at ease with himself as a public figure in a way he never could project as a candidate. People are different when the pressure is off. Bush will be a Carter, I suspect—somewhat exonerated in defeat. And when he begins doing television interviews again, I think he'll be terrific.

Which brings me to my Christmas wish for next year.

Bob Englehart, The Hartford Courant.

Disconnected

ALMOST EVERY DAY I eat lunch at Duke Zeibert's, sometimes dinner, too. There's always a box of matzo and some butter substitute waiting at my table. My diet was restricted after a 1987 heart attack, and Duke knows what I can and cannot eat. He says he's my surrogate father and takes good care of me. So why cook?

Duke's is perfectly located in the center of northwest Washington, in a modern glass office building on the corner of L Street and Connecticut Avenue. One street over, influential lawyers and lobbyists prowl the "K Street Corridor." Prominent think tanks, like the conservative American Enterprise Institute and the left-leaning Brookings Institution, have offices nearby, as do many news organizations. *Time*'s Washington bureau is upstairs. The *Wall Street Journal,* ABC News, the *Washington Post,* CBS, and National

Public Radio are all within walking distance. The White House and the Capitol are only a short cab ride away.

Looking up from my salad on any given day, I might see ABC's David Brinkley or *Post* Chairman Katharine Graham and her publisher son, Don. I see former Bush aide Margaret Tutwiler lunching with Democratic godfather Robert Strauss, the former ambassador to Russia. I say hello to the *Wall Street Journal*'s Al Hunt. I shake hands with Mark Shields, the Democratic analyst, and Ed Rollins, the Republican political consultant. Top government officials and members of Congress pass by. There's Tip O'Neill, the former Speaker of the House. There's Bill Bennett, the former education secretary and drug czar. They eat Duke's matzo-ball soup, crab cakes, and onion bread. They wave and smile. They watch each other. They schmooze, chatter, pitch, and swing. It's the all-star game. Great fun, and everyone is a friend.

Duke has fed presidents from Truman to Clinton. His restaurant is the capital at its clubby best, Washington's "Brown Derby." It is constantly abuzz with political chitchat: who's up, who's down, who's in, who's out. I love it, especially in election years. We're all political junkies at Duke's.

Going into the last campaign, however, I think I had a leg up on some of my fellow insiders. President Bush may have looked like a shoo-in for reelection, and 1992 may have seemed like it would be the most boring year in politics since, well, 1988. But the voters were restless. Something was brewing, and I could sense it—even without a poll.

For an hour every night on my radio show, carried nationally by Mutual Radio, I would open the phones to talk with my audience about anything that was on their minds. No guests or experts, just me and the listeners. We talked about sports and movies. They suggested guests and topics for future shows. Before the Gulf War, in 1991, they were nervous and divided. After the war they were euphoric. But when the euphoria began to fade, the nervousness came back. They were not anxious about a foreign enemy. They were worried about the future. They were nervous about the economy, crime, and the price of health care. And they were afraid no one in the government and no one running for office had answers for them. When one caller suggested I run for president, I knew we were in for a wacky year.

At CNN we wanted to capture some of this same voter angst on "Larry King Live." So in January 1992 we arranged to hold a televised town meeting in Pittsburgh. Pennsylvania would be a key state in the 1992 election. It leaned Republican historically, voting for Reagan twice and then Bush. The collapse of the coal and steel industries, however, shook Pennsylvania's economy. In November 1991 its disgruntled voters elected little-known Harris Wofford, a bookish Democrat and former college president, in a special Senate election. Wofford won by promising to reform the nation's health care system, beating Republican Richard Thornburgh, the former governor and Bush's attorney general. Thornburgh was heavily favored and resigned from the Bush administration to run, so his defeat was widely seen as a political warning to the president, who had campaigned hard for him.

Pittsburgh was an attractive site to us because its problems were typical. We wanted a normal American community with normal problems—and it was Tammy's hometown. Pittsburgh hadn't been hit as hard as many communities by the recession. Unemployment there that January was high—up a point from the previous winter to 7.3 percent—but it remained behind the national rate, then 8.0 percent.[1] Still, our audience of about two thousand at the city's Soldiers and Sailors Memorial Hall seemed to give faces to the anxious callers I'd heard from on my radio show.

Betty Esper, the mayor of nearby Homestead, told us how the steel industry's withdrawal from her community left the borough with no tax base to deal with its growing problems. "We have a police department we have to maintain, and with unemployment and drugs in the neighborhoods, we need our police department," she said. "What is the federal government planning to do to help the small communities who have to survive until the vacant land [the steel companies] used to occupy can be developed in this type of an economy?"

Some in our audience did not want to pay more taxes to solve such problems. "My taxes are eating me alive and killing me . . . ," a small businessman said. "I work until May just to pay personal income taxes. I work until July to pay increased state taxes and increased federal taxes on business. I work until . . . the end of September to pay my health insurance for the year, and then mid-October to pay the health insurance of others who work with me. . . . That gives me from the second week in October to the end of December to pay for the education of my children, my clothing, my car, etc. I can't stand the taxation anymore."

Some of what we heard from the audience that night was tragic, like the story of an unemployed steel worker who was sitting with his young daughter and son. "Are you getting unemployment insurance?" I asked.

"Yes, I am."

"Is that enough to take care of your basic needs?"

"Well," he said, "it's enough to take care of basic needs, but it's not enough to provide health care for your family. . . . I think it's a [sad] state of affairs when a doctor . . . tells you that the only thing that can save your wife is a transplant, but [he] can't recommend her to any hospital because you do not have any insurance."

I hated having to ask the next question. "Did that happen to you?" I said.

"Yes, it did."

"Did she die?"

"Yes she did."

Two thousand people were absolutely silent. Here was this nice man in his sweater and his glasses. It could be anyone. There were his kids, right there next to him. I wondered if viewers watching at home were as choked up as I was, as the crowd was. Or was it just another televised tale of woe, like so many we see every night on the news?

There were other sad stories, too, but most of what we heard in Pittsburgh seemed to come from a deep frustration with politics and those who practiced it. Why wasn't Washington doing anything? Or, more often, why can't Washington do anything? An out-of-work sales and marketing manager said he didn't think his elected officials would do much about unemployment because they cared more about saving their own jobs. "And in order to get the support to be reelected," he said, "you have to yield to so many PACs [political action committees] . . . that you can't take a stand. . . . Everything is a compromise."

"Don't you think, though, that the people in Washington— the congressmen, the president—want your vote?" I asked.

"Yeah," he said, "I think they want it, but . . . I'm not going to deliver a hundred thousand dollars to their campaigns."[2]

The marketing manager was not the only one to express such anger at his government that night. Those views were, in fact, sadly common, as a late-1991 survey by the Times Mirror Center for the People & the Press showed:

· Only 36 percent of those responding to the survey said elected officials cared about what they think.

· Less than 50 percent thought they had "any say about what the government does."

· And a whopping 84 percent said that "people in Washington lose touch with the people pretty quickly." Only 15 percent disagreed with that one.

After numbers like that, it was hardly surprising that about two-thirds of those surveyed in the Times Mirror Center poll said they were dissatisfied with the way things were going in their country.[3]

The public's general pessimism and frustration with government cut deep into Bush's popularity. The president's approval rating fell to 55 percent in the November 1991 survey—nearly 30 points below his post–Gulf War peak. By the time of our Pittsburgh town meeting in January, the president was at 46 percent.[4] Bush had done little to help himself. Many voters hadn't forgiven him for violating his mantralike campaign pledge: "Read my lips. No new taxes." Great election-year bravado, once upon a time. But by 1992 it was just a broken promise—nothing unusual from a politician.

Bush also fed the public's perception that Washington dwellers were "out of touch" by refusing for many months to acknowledge that the country was in a recession. In September 1990 economic growth was "slow," but we weren't in a recession. Four months later Bush said the recession would be a "shallow" one—"should it be proved technically that this country is in a recession." In June 1991 the recession had "lasted perhaps longer than we would have thought" but was not "as deep as many [had] predicted." In October the economy was still "recovering."[5] The president was practically writing an advertisement for his opponents.

Bush, an economics major from Yale, had a point. Economists define recessions as back-to-back quarters of negative growth, which wasn't exactly the case in the United States at the time. But, as I often say—and as Bush conceded when I interviewed him at the White House the following October—when you're out of work it's a depression. You don't care what the economists call it. People wanted their president's sympathy—and a little action—not semantics.

"I could have handled that better," Bush told me.[6]

Bush wasn't the only incumbent who was having trouble with the voters. At the other end of Pennsylvania Avenue, Congress was on probation, too. The public forgot the eloquent House and Senate debates on using force to drive Iraq from Kuwait even faster than they forgot Bush's Gulf War victory. Scandals, perks, and pay raises seemed to hurt many members of both chambers. Once-unassailable incumbents, such as Senator Bill Bradley, a New Jersey Democrat, faced tougher-than-expected challenges in the 1990 elections. Even more seemed at risk in 1992, especially after the mother of all congressional scandals—the check-bouncing scam at the House bank.

The checks in the check-bouncing scandal didn't actually

bounce. In fact, the House bank wasn't actually a bank. It was more like a credit union, through which members of the House could deposit money and write checks. In late 1991 a report by the General Accounting Office (GAO) found that hundreds of current and former members had abused their check-writing privileges, routinely exceeding their balances without any penalties. No taxpayer funds were involved, but these "kiters" enraged the public, as we found out when Congressman Bob Mrazek from New York came on our show in mid-March to explain his nine-hundred-plus overdrafts. "I'm in the armed forces . . . ," an angry caller from Virginia Beach told the Manhattan Democrat. "If I write a bad check or my wife writes a bad check, I'm in trouble. I can get fired. What makes it right for you?"

Mrazek, then a candidate in New York's Democratic Senate primary, apologized, "I have made a pledge that any policy that is not available to any of my constituents I will never accept again in the future."[7] But for this promising young member of the House, the damage was done. Mrazek told our viewers he would remain a candidate but pulled out of the Senate race a short while later.

Many members of Congress decided not to face their constituents' wrath and sat out the 1992 campaign. In the House a record sixty-five members retired or did not seek reelection in order to run for another office. In the Senate eight members gave up their seats without a fight. Two of the more prominent retirees from the Senate were New Hampshire's Warren B. Rudman, a two-term Republican, and Colorado's Timothy E. Wirth, a first-term Democrat. Both were active reformers on Capitol Hill. Wirth was a "Watergate baby," whose constituents first sent him to Washington as a representative with the reform-minded House class of 1974.

Rudman had cosponsored the Gramm-Rudman-Hollings deficit reduction package in 1985 and was still fighting budget battles when he announced that he would retire at the end of the term.

Rudman and Wirth appeared on our show together in late June and, like many Congressional retirees, sounded as frustrated with Washington as any voter ever polled. "If I thought that I could have a major impact here in the next six years, I would have run for reelection," Rudman told me. But "I've watched the gridlock develop here, the divided government, the failure to tell the American people the truth, the inability of the political system to work, the deficits growing out of control. . . ."

"The failure of who to tell the truth?" I asked.

"The failure of both political parties; of presidents for, really, the last eighteen years as far as I'm concerned; of leaders of both parties and, frankly, members of Congress, to tell the American people that there is no such thing as a free lunch and we're heading up upon the reefs."

Wirth said he had felt an obligation to run again. "And then," he said, "there comes a time when you say to yourself—or I did to myself—Hey, I'm becoming angry enough at this process. I'm becoming in elected office somebody I don't like. This process of raising money and going through very negative campaigns is just eating on me, and it's time for some new growth to come in."

Not the usual sort of talk voters were used to from their legislators. Our audience, however, hardly thought Rudman and Wirth's decisions to leave politics were heroic. Their questions that night were as pointed as ever. One viewer in Butte, Montana, phoned in to ask "why all these congressmen that are retiring are not going to leave their congressional campaign funds there [for] the budget." The next caller, from New Orleans, wanted to know if either of our guests planned to "use his contacts and his insider information to work as a lobbyist after leaving office." A viewer from Albany, New York, asked "how the Congress can ask the middle class to tighten its belt when they keep voting themselves perks—high salaries, unlimited accumulation of annual leave." A Texan asked the senators if they were willing to trim their "extremely generous congressional retirement benefits" to reduce the deficit. "This is a sincerity check from a skeptical voter out here," that caller said.[8]

No exoneration that night. Retiring wasn't good enough; voters wanted the satisfaction of slamming the door behind "career politicians" like Wirth and Rudman.

Sometimes I think our viewers can be a little rabid, dismissing everyone who comes to Washington as corrupt. I can see why they might feel that way. But I have met and interviewed many politicians in my career, and most of them—even members of Congress—are honest men and women who want to serve their constituents and improve the country. When I introduce the public to their leaders and representatives on the air, I always hope they can see what I see. Lately, though, that has not been the case.

Voter anger has fueled a national movement to limit congressional terms. By the end of the 1992 campaign, voters in fifteen states had approved initiatives limiting the terms of their congressmen and senators. Bush and Quayle plugged the idea in their campaign in hopes of clearing the way for Republican congressional challenges, only to find themselves swept off the stage by the same anti-incumbent mood.

Polls show that roughly three-quarters of the public support term limits, but I do not. I think elections are the best way to limit terms. I am aware of all the arguments for term limits, and I am just as disturbed as their proponents by how difficult it is to challenge an incumbent. Even in an anti-incumbent election year such as 1992, for instance, only forty-three members of the House of Representatives who were running for reelection lost (nineteen in the primaries and twenty-three in the fall). But I would much rather change the way candidates raise and spend campaign funds than give up my right to vote for someone I think is doing a good job. Of course, opposing term limits is hard for a person who makes his career in Washington on TV and on the radio. So many people think the media are as much a part of the problem as the politicians. Democratic presidential candidate Jerry Brown, a vocal term-limits advocate, even jokingly suggested term limits for the media—including talk-show hosts—during an interview on "Donahue."[9] Did Brown know an applause line or what?

Wirth did not get a lot of applause from our viewers that night in June, but the senator did make an interesting point about the press, which he said bore some responsibility for Washington's failings. "I've been running for public office for eighteen years," Wirth said, "have had difficult elections, always had tough times getting elected. And that's part of the process. That's fine. But in the process of these elections, I have never had—not once that I can remember—a reasonable conversation with any member of the press who . . . was knowledgeable about the budget issue and the deficit."[10]

Wirth's comment was interesting to me because it was such a common complaint among politicians and the public. The press has never been one of this nation's most popular institutions, especially in hard times. Shooting the messenger is nothing new in politics. But as voters' frustrations with politics-as-usual increased, so did the public's frustration with the traditional media. "When people hold the president and Congress in low esteem, the press sinks as well," says Tim Russert, moderator of NBC's "Meet the Press."[11] That unhappiness, perhaps more than anything else, led to the talk-show revolution.

By 1992 CNN and C-SPAN were changing the way the public consumed news, and that was changing the relationship between journalists and their viewers or readers in profound ways. Round-the-clock, blow-by-blow live coverage meant people could watch news happen, unfiltered. John Sununu, now a cohost of CNN's "Crossfire," says that phenomenon created a "chasm" between the public and journalists. The public "can see Congress in action on C-SPAN, can see press conferences covered live . . . [and] wars live on CNN," Sununu says. "Therefore, when they turn to CBS, NBC, and ABC, a lot more of them are saying, 'That's not what I saw today. Why are these guys saying this?' "[12]

Interactive shows like "Larry King Live" give viewers a chance to serve as remote-control reporters. They can interview newsmakers themselves and comment on events as they watch them. Audience-participation programs also allow viewers to serve as editors and producers. Callers can set or change the agenda to some extent. And, in some cases, they can even rein in some of the media's worst excesses. Mandy Grunwald, an early talk-show proponent in the Democratic campaign, says 1992 was "a year where people were fed up with political rhetoric, didn't want a lot of bullshit, didn't want to get manipulated. And so the unvarnished settings, the settings where they could judge for themselves, were the settings they trusted most." [13]

Republican party chairman Rich Bond recognized this trend, too, even if it took him a while to explain it to his nominee. "I remember describing this phenomenon to President Bush during the campaign, and my theory was that people were listening [to the media] differently," Bond says. "And they were so alienated from the national establishments of conventional media and conventional politics that they would believe more what was said on a 'Larry King' show than they would believe what George Will said on 'David Brinkley.' " [14]

Many in the press resented the call-in shows for this very reason. I think some reporters felt our callers were treading on their turf. But the press's unhappiness wasn't too surprising. There had been a similar reaction among journalists fifteen years earlier, in March 1977, when President Jimmy Carter answered audience phone calls for two hours in the Oval Office on the CBS Radio Network and PBS. Writing about the program in the following Sunday's *Washington Post,* Sander Vanocur criticized CBS anchor Walter Cronkite for agreeing to serve as "master of ceremonies" and moderate the program.

"It is quite a different role than the one in which Cronkite asks for and is granted an interview with the president," Vanocur said. "That is a perfectly proper journalistic exercise. But on the telephone call-in, Cronkite was not functioning in the role of journalist. He was part of the White House propaganda machinery." [15]

I've heard that before.

The Washington press corps has "a really important role to play" in the political process, says Jeff Zucker, who was executive producer for NBC's "Today" show during the campaign. "But the fact is they did become a little obsolete, and that's because they made themselves out of touch," he adds. "They would say, 'Well, it's up to us to make sure that the questions Joe Voter isn't asking get asked because those are important issues.' There's something to that. But they take themselves a little too seriously. . . . [T]here's something to this whole idea [that] ever since Watergate, the Washington press corps [has been] trying to play a game of 'gotcha.' " [16]

Perhaps no form of "gotcha" journalism irritates voters more than the way campaign reporters delve into politician's private lives—even when the public has a legitimate interest in those stories. Many journalists are just as uncomfortable with this sort of prying as is the public. But, as Larry J. Sabato has documented in his 1991 book *Feeding Frenzy,* competitive pressures often seem to produce "lowest-common-denominator" reporting, in which the slimiest, sleaziest accounts or rumors can explode into major scandals. Under these rules any story is fair game once it has appeared in print or on the air somewhere—no matter how scurrilous the source.[17] We certainly weren't immune to that at "Larry King Live." I often delve into personality and character questions. I want to know what someone's life is like. But maybe we all went too far in 1992.

Historically the public has relied on journalists' judgment to determine what information is newsworthy and what is not. And the public hasn't minded all that much. Who wants to skim through the hundreds of pages published in the *Congressional Record* every day? But the "rules" journalists use in deciding what to cover have changed drastically since Watergate.

When I was growing up, for instance, we had no idea that

President Franklin D. Roosevelt was wheelchair bound because the press never revealed that fact. It was wartime, and reporters felt an obligation then to protect the public from pictures of their crippled leader. Should we turn back the clocks? The level of education among journalists is much higher today than it was then, but I'm not sure I'd want to trust today's reporters with that sort of responsibility. I'd rather know.

On the other hand the media never exposed John F. Kennedy's alleged extramarital affairs when he was in office. We certainly enjoyed sharing stories about those affairs among ourselves and with other political figures.[18] But many of the White House reporters who gossiped about the president's liaisons also played up scenes of Kennedy with his wife and children that made him seem like a devoted family man. After watching the frenzied coverage of Clinton's personal life thirty-two years later, it's hard to say whether that was good or bad.

Rumors about Clinton's marital problems predated the Arkansas governor's presidential campaign. They were even the subject of a lot of Washington party chatter when he announced that he would not be a candidate for president four years earlier, two months after the *Miami Herald* helped Gary Hart end his candidacy. At the time Clinton said he wanted to spend more time with his wife, Hillary, and their daughter, Chelsea.[19] The Clintons hoped to put the rumors about their marriage to rest when they attended a breakfast meeting with reporters in the fall of 1991. The couple acknowledged that their marriage had not been perfect but said they had worked out their problems. It was their business, they told the reporters, and they thought it should stay that way. And it did, more or less, until the following January.

That month the *Star,* a weekly supermarket tabloid, paid Gennifer Flowers to tell the story of her alleged twelve-year affair with Clinton. Flowers, a state employee and sometime lounge singer in Little Rock, was already familiar to many campaign reporters, some of whom had even been to Arkansas to check out rumors about her and the governor. Flowers had denied the rumors in the past, and most reporters were apparently satisfied that she was telling the truth—at least until her *Star* interview.

I missed Bill and Hillary Clinton's denials on a special edition of "60 Minutes" on January 26. It aired right after the Super Bowl, and I was at the game. But many Americans met their next president that night on CBS. Clinton denied ever having an affair with Flowers but acknowledged that there had been problems in his marriage. Interviewer Steve Croft asked what that meant, but Clinton would not elaborate. "I think the American people, at least people that have been married for a long time, know what it means and know the whole range of things that it can mean . . .," he said. "I have acknowledged wrongdoing, I have acknowledged causing pain in my marriage. I have said things to you tonight and to the American people from the beginning that no American politician ever has. I think most Americans who are watching this tonight, they'll know what we're saying. They'll get it."[20]

The following day Flowers answered reporters' questions at a news conference in New York. She also played tapes of phone conversations between her and Clinton that she said corroborated her story. It was not one of journalism's finest moments. Had Clinton used a condom? one reporter asked. Had she slept with any other presidential candidates? It was ridiculous, but too titillating to ignore. With the *Star,* "60 Minutes," and a nationally televised news conference, Flowers's tell-all "revelations" became big news, even bigger than Bush's long-awaited State of the Union address the following night. No wonder Bush was having such a hard time getting his message out.

At "Larry King Live" we joined the Flowers frenzy on the day of her New York news conference. Our guests that night included Rod Lurie, an expert on tabloids; David Osborne, a friend of Clinton's; and *New York Post* gossip columnist Cindy Adams, whose stories about the *Star*'s account helped turn Flowers's tale into "legitimate" news. "If he bedded someone, that's fine," Adams told me. "It seems that's a national pastime with people who are either presidents or running for president."[21]

We certainly got some heat for that show. *Los Angeles Times* media critic Howard Rosenberg criticized me for letting Adams ramble unchallenged about other women who claimed to have had affairs with Clinton.[22] "There's a whole pack of them out there that are sending in information," Adams had said. "I simply haven't used it because until now, until he started to run, I didn't care a hoot in hell for Clinton of Arkansas. . . . Suddenly, we all care."[23] Syndicated columnist Cal Thomas repeated Adams's charge, attributing it to our show, on ABC's "Nightline" later in the evening.[24]

I certainly did not want to spread unsubstantiated stories about a presidential candidate. Should I have challenged Adams to produce some sort of evidence, as Rosenberg suggested? Probably. Should they have talked about it later on "Nightline"? Probably not. But that is how a feeding frenzy works. Flowers's story was a Pandora's box, and none of us in the media felt we could close it. I certainly thought Clinton was in trouble, maybe even mortally wounded. The woman had a tape, after all. That was pretty convincing to me, but maybe she had set him up.

I also had mixed feelings about the charges that Clinton briefly joined and then quit an ROTC unit to avoid the draft during the Vietnam War—a story that surfaced in the following weeks. Maybe that's because, as a public person, I've had parts of my own life dragged through newsprint and plastered over supermarket checkout counters more often than I would like. My last divorce got so much ink that Bush even asked me about it when we saw each other at an Orioles game.

The public had mixed feelings about the Flowers and draft stories, too. After Clinton's second-place showing in February's New Hampshire primary, 64 percent of those surveyed in a national poll by the Times Mirror Center said the draft and Flowers controversies made no difference to them. But 56 percent told the Times Mirror Center that they thought it was important for voters to learn about these cases, and 59 percent thought the press had handled the matters responsibly.[25] So the press kept the stories alive, with question after question about Clinton's character and personal life.

But the reporters' interest in these questions outlasted the public's. In all four of Clinton's appearances on our show in 1992, only one of thirty callers asked him a so-called character question—in this case, one about his draft record. At NBC's "Today," producer Zucker had a similar experience when Clinton answered viewer calls on his show in June. Zucker even remembers turning around in the control room to specifically ask his crew if any callers had questions about affairs or Clinton's character. No one did.[26]

"The callers cared a lot more about issues than we . . . [gave]

them credit for," Zucker says. Questions about Clinton's character were "a legitimate issue," but "there does come a point where his tax plan matters more . . . ," he adds. "We care a lot more about Gennifer Flowers than Joe Voter in Dubuque, Iowa."[27]

Donahue found this out the hard way, when his audience actually booed him for pressing Clinton on Flowers's charges during an interview in April. Clinton recognized early in the show that the crowd was on his side and craftily turned Donahue's questions against him—and the rest of his media tormentors. "We're going to sit here a long time in silence, Phil," the candidate said. "I'm not going to answer any more of these questions. I've answered them until I'm blue in the face. You are responsible for the cynicism in this country. You don't want to talk about the real issues."

When Donahue went to his audience for questions, they turned on him, too. "Given the pathetic state of most of the United States at this point . . . I can't believe you spent half an hour of air time attacking this man's character," said the first woman to whom he offered his microphone. "I'm not even a Bill Clinton supporter, but I think this is ridiculous." The audience applauded.[28] I knew Clinton was home free when I saw the woman's comment on the news that night.

Donahue thinks the adultery question was an important one and that he had an obligation to pursue it, no matter how his audience or the public at large felt. "Our job is not to be popular . . . ," he says. "You have a responsibility to ask questions that don't necessarily endear you" to your audience. Nevertheless Donahue was a little embarrassed by the booing. "I mean, I knew my mother was watching," he says.[29]

On our show we tried to take our cues on this matter from

our viewers. Later in the year Flowers posed for *Penthouse* and told the magazine intimate details about her alleged affair with the governor. To promote the issue the magazine called my producers and offered Flowers as a guest. We declined, and I'm glad.

As the campaign wore on and Clinton racked up victories in the primaries, the mainstream press caught on, too. The public knew what it needed to know on this subject. That was clear from the booing on "Donahue" and even from the sorts of questions callers were asking—and, more important, not asking. Interactive television served as an emergency brake on the runaway coverage of Clinton's personal life.

So what *did* our audience want to talk about? About half of the 122 viewers who phoned in with questions for the six major presidential and vice presidential candidates asked about issues. Forty-six questions were on domestic policy: the economy (eleven), defense (five), taxes (four), the budget (three), and so on. The rest were mostly political—questions about running mates, the campaign itself, and the like. Only four were about the candidates' backgrounds or personal lives.

The obsessive focus of the campaign press on personality is not the only way reporters seemed out of touch to voters—as out of touch, in fact, as politicians. Clinton campaign strategist James Carville saw this disconnect in the meager coverage of most Americans' declining incomes. "Most people who cover [political] races . . . frankly don't know anybody who hasn't had any income growth, so they tend to be more immersed in other things . . . ," he says. "So people are . . . saying, 'When is somebody going to ask something that matters to me and talk about something that matters to me?' "

And, as Carville points out, the insulated world of the media and politicians—and of professional campaign strategists enjoying "five thousand percent pay raises"—is not always the best place from which to track the concerns of average voters. "It's a loop," he says. "And it's not bad people. It's not a sinister sort of conspiracy and that we're all in this sort of cabal together. . . . But a just man sins seven times a day. I mean, it's so easy to forget."[30]

Washington Post columnist David Broder has described this same "loop" many times. Consultants "have become for those of us in political journalism not only our best sources but, in many cases, our best friends," he said in a 1991 speech.

> We have a lot in common with each other, the consultants and the political reporters. We are all drawn to our work by our love of the gossip and maneuver and individual idiosyncrasies that make politics such a fascinating game for the insider. . . . In our candid moments, the consultants and the political journalists would also confess that we share a sense of superiority even to the candidates. . . . We feel superior to them because we know that while they have everything at stake in a particular election, we have the kind of franchise that lets us play this game over and over again. The day after the election, political reporters start thinking about the next campaign, and so do the campaign consultants. We are the permanent part of the political establishment, if you will.[31]

I know exactly what Broder was talking about. I see it every day at lunch. But shows like ours give voters a place in that loop, a voice in their own political process. Call-in shows are the media equivalent of a table at Duke Zeibert's.

Welcome to the establishment. Pass the matzo.

Jeff Parker, Sunshine Statements Feature Services.
Reprinted with permission.

Cue the Talent

THE FIRST PERSON I ever voted for was Adlai E. Stevenson, the losing Democratic presidential candidate in 1952 and 1956. He was a hero of mine, and I was thrilled when I had a chance to interview him on the radio in Miami early in my career. I told him I was a supporter and gushed as I tried to explain what an honor it was for me to be talking with him. "Mr. King," Stevenson said, "we have never met. Yet when I walked into the room tonight, I said to my companion, 'I have a feeling this man is one of the great judges of character we will ever meet.' How unfortunate that there weren't ten million more of you."[1]

Stevenson would have been a great guest on "Larry King Live." I will always measure candidates and politicians against him. It takes certain telegenic qualities to win over our viewers, but it is

not so simple—or as phony—as some blow-dried, phrase-turning
politicians think. Quotable nuggets are fine for someone feeding
hungry campaign journalists with deadlines to meet and limited
space to fill. That's why most political reporters ask such predictable questions: Are you going to run? What do you think of the
latest polls? Voters, "real people," are not predictable. It takes
humor, intelligence, charm, and charisma to answer them in extended sessions on live television. So Stevenson's incredible blue
eyes might have dazzled us on our color sets, but on a call-in show,
his boundless, crafty wit would have been an even more important
feature.

"Every thinking person will vote for you," an enthusiastic supporter once told him after a speech.

"That's not enough, madam," Stevenson said. "We need a majority."[2]

When Stevenson made remarks like that as a presidential candidate, he was criticized for being an "egghead" who spoke over
the heads of the public. But today's electorate would have loved
his sharp wit and tell-it-like-it-is manner.

Mario M. Cuomo may be the closest thing to an Adlai Stevenson we have in politics today. Unfortunately he decided not to run
for president in 1992. Cuomo is the only politician I've ever met
who is as smooth dodging questions as he is answering them. During an interview at Madison Square Garden during the 1992 Democratic National Convention, I asked the New York governor if he
would serve in a Clinton administration. Cuomo shrugged. "I would
like to be a talk-show host," he said, "but there's a monopoly on
that job right now—between you and Sununu."[3]

Cuomo would have been a great call-in candidate, in part

because he has always understood the value of talk shows to people in his line of work. He has hosted state-wide radio call-in shows regularly in New York since he was first elected lieutenant govenor in the late 1970s. Why? "The sense of accessibility, the nexus, the connection between you and the people is very important," he explains. "You [have to] keep a connection with the people. . . . They feel better if they think they can reach their government, and you learn from hearing from them."[4]

Programmed candidates who can turn out nine-second sound bites like robots won't cut it with call-in viewers. Our audience wants serious answers to their questions. But they want to see a real person, too. In a way, shows like ours—on which candidates can ramble and interact with real people at some length—let voters measure a candidate's sincerity.

"The television camera really is a kind of personality X-ray machine," says Vice President Al Gore—borrowing a phrase from Thomas E. Dewey, the losing Republican presidential candidate in 1948. "Over time," Gore says, "the character of the individuals being judged by the American people will be more or less accurately assessed" through television.[5]

How much has television changed politics and politicians? It's a fun question. Abraham Lincoln mastered sound bites early, fitting his Gettysburg Address on an envelope. Thomas Jefferson, on the other hand, stuttered and did not like public speaking. How would either of them have done on a talk show? "Would a guy with wooden teeth have looked good on the 'Larry King' show?" asks Cuomo. And "does that mean George Washington couldn't win [an election] if there were Larry King?"[6]

The 1960 presidential election was the first won and lost on

television, and its victor, John F. Kennedy, was the original telegenic candidate. Consciously or unconsciously, many modern politicians have imitated Kennedy, from Democrats like Gary Hart to
Republicans such as former housing secretary Jack Kemp and House
Minority Whip Newt Gingrich.

In 1992 C-SPAN reran Kennedy's 1960 debates with then–
Vice President Richard M. Nixon, his Republican opponent.
Watching them three decades later, I remembered hearing the first
one on my car radio, driving from Orlando to Miami. The debate
was staid by current standards. There was no "Where's the beef?"
or "There you go again," or "Senator, you're no Jack Kennedy."[7]
It was a thoughtful debate about the issues between two bright,
knowledgeable guys—a tie, I remember thinking. But when I got
to the radio station to go on the air in Miami, it was unanimous.
Everyone there said Kennedy had won hands down. They had
watched the debate on television, and on TV Nixon looked fraz-
zled and shifty. Maybe it was the lighting or the makeup, as Nixon's campaign suggested—an early example of the type of damage
control political professionals now call "spin." Or maybe the TV
audience got an insight into the real Nixon that night. There was
a reason his successful campaigns for president in 1968 and 1972
were staged so carefully.

"There is little correlation between the qualities that make a
good leader and those that make a good TV performer . . . ,"
Nixon warned in his 1990 memoir, *In the Arena*. "TV undoubt-
edly disqualifies some who have leadership quality but no star
quality."[8]

I'm not sure if Paul Tsongas proved Nixon's rule or defied it.
The untelegenic former senator from Massachusetts did not win

the Democratic presidential nomination in 1992, but he did beat expectations and a virtual news blackout to become Bill Clinton's most serious challenger in the primaries.

As Tsongas himself will admit, he is hardly charismatic. "I called myself Kennedyesque," he says, "but nobody believed it, including my wife, children, best friends, and entire campaign staff."[9] But the camera—and the public—liked him, despite his lisp, puffy eyes, and funny voice. And that is a quality that is hard for pundits, or even talk-show hosts, to measure. You can't bottle it, you can't manufacture it, you can't patent it, but Tsongas had it.

I liked Tsongas and regret that we did not invite him to appear on our show as a candidate in 1992. We did not have him on as a guest until late April, after he withdrew from the presidential race. But like a lot of people in the media and in politics, I was slow to take his candidacy seriously. When he became the first Democrat to discuss challenging Bush in early 1991, the incumbent president's approval rating was at its post–Gulf War peak—around 80 or 90 percent in most polls.

The only people who told me to pay attention to Tsongas were both in the Bush administration, and I just thought they were being nice—or trying to build up a rival whom they thought would be easy prey in the fall. One was White House Chief of Staff Sununu, the former governor of New Hampshire, who reminded me that Tsongas had never lost an election in Massachusetts. The other was Vice President Dan Quayle, whom I asked about Tsongas in a May 1991 interview. "You know, Larry, a lot of people sort of write off Paul Tsongas . . . ," Quayle said. "I know people are saying that he's not qualified and that he's a lightweight and he's not substantive. But let me tell you, they don't know Senator

Tsongas like I do. He's a very substantive person. He's been underestimated his entire political life. . . . Don't write off Paul Tsongas. He's a very capable individual." [10]

One thing that helped Tsongas break through the media-imposed blackout that proceeded his victory in the New Hampshire primary was his sense of humor. I never knew how funny he was until a roast for Democratic Party Chairman Ron Brown in January 1992, a month before the kickoff primary. I was the emcee and introduced Tsongas, who proceeded to steal the show. "You know, I am a presidential candidate," he said. "I got into this race when George Bush was at 91 percent. Look what I've done to him. I have served my country." He gestured at me. "And this son of a bitch won't invite me on his program." [11]

As it turned out Quayle and Sununu were right about Tsongas. He was a battler and a stayer and, if his campaign had not run out of money, he might have pulled off a remarkable political upset and won his party's nomination. He would have had a lot of support from Republicans and from the business community. And his emphasis on reducing the deficit and rebuilding the U.S. manufacturing base might have kept Perot on the sidelines.

Tsongas, who suspended his indebted candidacy on March 19, felt enough of an affinity with Perot on economic matters that he not only considered endorsing the Texas billionaire but even contemplated running with him. Perot never extended such an invitation, but after the primaries he and an adviser did meet secretly with Tsongas and his campaign manager, Dennis Kanin, in a Connecticut hotel room. In vice presidential mating rituals, this was a first date, but Tsongas left the meeting uncomfortable with Perot's temperament.

"We talked about the lack of money," Tsongas says, "and he asked me if I were to run again, how would I avoid the problem. And the straight answer, obviously, is that, well, I'm known now, and I'd be taken seriously by the press. Therefore we would have the money. But instead I said, 'Actually, I intend to ask you to adopt me.' And what I remember about that was Dennis and I both laughed, and we were the only ones laughing in the room." [12]

Classic Tsongas. We should have had him on the show.

Tsongas was most comfortable campaigning when he could be himself. Reading speeches, he was stiff and unconvincing. But in debates or interviews, he was warm, smart, and funny. He was human. He interwove explanations of his economic proposals with descriptions of the commitment he felt to his three children and their generation—a commitment that he said developed fully after his dramatic battle with a usually fatal form of cancer. Tsongas had left the Senate in 1984 after one term when he was diagnosed with lymphoma. He survived an experimental bone marrow transplant that he said cured him. As a candidate Tsongas said the painful and frightening experience left him with questions about his mortality and his legacy. What sort of country will we leave our children? he asked recession-weary voters. His answer, an eighty-five-page economic manifesto, came from his own story of recovery and renewal. They were linked.

But if cancer gave Tsongas the passion to win voters over, it might have cost him the election, had he beaten Clinton and become his party's nominee in the fall. Shortly after Tsongas suspended his candidacy, the *New York Times* ran a front-page story suggesting that the candidate had misled the public about his recovery by not revealing treatment he received the year after his marrow transplant. Tsongas angrily denied the *Times* report, pointing out that he had discussed that treatment in earlier interviews. In August 1992, however, his doctors found another growth. A biopsy performed in November, just two weeks after the election, showed it was cancerous and required chemotherapy.[13] During the transition period between the election and the inauguration, Tsongas was hospitalized twice for complications related to the treatment.[14]

Stories about a possible recurrence of cancer probably would have destroyed his candidacy. But if Tsongas had won, pictures of a president-elect undergoing chemotherapy would have frightened the public, probably unleashing a massive feeding frenzy. Should he have known? Could he have known? Did he lie? Should we care? It would be talk-show mania, with doctors and patients and constitutional scholars debating the ramifications and possibilities. He might have had to step aside even before the inauguration. But he would have fought first with the same wit and character he used to get his underrated candidacy noticed in the first place. "The last living cell that will die in my body is the desire to be president of the United States," he said at the late-November news conference at which he confirmed press reports about his cancer. "And there is no treatment for it."[15]

Tsongas had no trouble sharing his feelings with the public, unlike another Greek from Massachusetts, Gov. Michael S. Dukakis, the losing Democratic nominee in 1988. Dukakis seemed like a machine to many voters, a passionless pol who promised to bring "competence," not "ideology," to the presidency. But the public does not want to send an "iceman" to the White House. They want their leaders to have blood coursing through them. They want to see tears and anger and emotion—things Dukakis wasn't willing, or able, to share with them. That's why CNN anchor Bernard Shaw's first question to Dukakis during a 1988 debate with then–Vice President Bush hurt the governor so much: "Governor, if Kitty Dukakis were raped and murdered, would you favor an irrevocable death penalty for the killer?"

"No, I [wouldn't], Bernard," Dukakis said stiffly, "and I think you know that I've opposed the death penalty during all of my life. I think there are better and more effective ways to deal with violent crime," which he then tried to explain.[16]

The problem for Dukakis was that the public didn't want to hear about the most "effective" ways of dealing with violent crime, even if they agreed with his arguments.

For some reason shows like ours seem to be good places for candidates to showcase this side of themselves. The Dukakis campaign, to its credit, recognized that eventually—but probably too late in the campaign to make much of a difference. He and Kitty Dukakis came on "Larry King Live" as guests in late October 1988. "My family has felt the pain of crime," he said, when I asked him if Shaw's question had thrown him. "You know, my dad was a young immigrant who came here, became a doctor, and was practicing medicine. When he was seventy-seven years of age, he was bound and gagged and beaten by an intruder who was looking for drugs. My only brother was killed by a hit-and-run driver who we've always assumed was on drugs or drunk. So I know the pain of it."[17] Where was *that* answer at the debate nine days earlier?

We also saw a chemistry between the governor and Kitty Dukakis on our show that night—an almost visible sexual energy that helped humanize him with our viewers. "I haven't seen you in seven days," he said when she walked on to the set to join us during a commercial break.

"Eight," she said.

I repeated the exchange to our audience. "This is a love affair," I said. "Right? Ongoing?"

"For twenty-five years," he cooed. "It gets better all the time." [18]

It was smart of the Dukakis campaign to have them on together because Kitty Dukakis always seemed to bring out this side of her husband, as she had during a St. Patrick's Day parade in Chicago earlier in the year. "Tonight if I'm asleep, wake me up," Dukakis had whispered to her during the celebration. "Don't let a moment go by." The governor was whispering into an open microphone, but he didn't seem to mind. [19]

"I wouldn't have married him if he weren't passionate," Kitty Dukakis explained to me during our interview. But "his passion gets translated into programs. . . ."

"Why does he project the image that was the opposite of what we saw here tonight?" I asked.

"I think oftentimes first generation Americans . . . are taught when they're young that those kinds of emotions are left at home for the people they're close to and those they love . . . ," she said. "I mean, this is a man who has been there every step of the way for me. . . . When I made a decision to confront my dependency [on amphetamines], Michael didn't think about his own reelection and being hurt by that. He thought about me, and said I was much more important to him than an election." [20]

Kitty Dukakis was very open with us that night about her fight to kick a diet-pill habit. But like most of her campaign staff—and apparently her husband, too—I had no idea that she had developed an alcohol problem. As she explained a year later in her autobiography, *Now You Know,* that problem became unmanageable for her after the election. She would cancel her appointments each day, close the curtains, and drink alone in her kitchen or bedroom until she passed out. Finally, summoned by her son one afternoon, Dukakis "rushed home to rouse his wife and lovingly, tenderly, removed the filthy clothing, washed the vomitus from her body, and cleaned up the mess."[21] Clearly Michael Dukakis was not the cold fish the public thought they had seen when Shaw asked his question at the debate with Bush. But, right or wrong, the public wants to see that side of a candidate before they are willing to give him or her the keys to the White House.

That's a lesson Bill Clinton's campaign learned well and put to use as they reintroduced their candidate to the American public in a blitz of talk-show and call-in appearances in June 1992 — on our show, the broadcast networks, MTV, and "The Arsenio Hall Show." "Thanks to you, Larry, and to the other programs that I've been invited on, I've been able to relate to people in a way that I can't if I'm just dependent on eight-second sound bites on the evening news . . . ," Clinton told me during his second appearance on our show that month. "You have to reach out to all of America every day. And they have to see you and get a feel for what your commitments are, what you care about, what's in it that's much bigger than anybody's personal ambition. . . . So that's what I'm here for."[22]

Clinton had no problem talking about himself. He even liked to use his own stories to empathize with his questioners. On "CBS This Morning" in June he took questions from studio audiences in New York and five other cities. A laboratory technician in

Connecticut asked Clinton what he would do to help single mothers like her. "This is a very personal thing with me," Clinton said. "I was born to a single mother. My father was killed in a car wreck shortly before I was born, and she went back to nursing school and got to a point where she could support me. This is a major issue with me personally."[23]

Talk about bonding. Clinton could have simply given the woman his however-many-point plan for providing job training to welfare mothers, which is exactly what he did next. But by starting his answer the way he did, he was telling the audience—in the studio and at home—that he appreciated all his mom had done for him. They had struggled for what they had, he said, without saying it. This was Clinton's get-to-know-me-better strategy at work. I assumed, for instance, that was why Clinton's campaign had his mother, colorful Virginia Kelley, phone in from Nevada during a show in early October.

"We're at the Clinton/Gore headquarters," Kelley said when her son asked what she was doing in Las Vegas.

"That's your story, mother, and you stick to it as long as we're on the air," Clinton said. "You're just out there helping our campaign."[24]

My respect for Clinton, especially for his abilities as a campaigner, increased during the election year. Clinton has a remarkable ability to remember factoids and statistics, which roll out of him like gum balls whenever you put a penny in and ask him to explain his position on an issue. Sometimes it is impressive. Sometimes it is dizzying—especially when his position has evolved or changed, as often seems to be the case.

I was dubious about Clinton throughout the primaries, as was much of the public. But he grew on me as I watched him campaign from talk show to talk show after the primaries ended. I was impressed by the way he looked people in the eye and listened to them. Even Ronald Reagan's longtime image guru, Michael K. Deaver, had to marvel. "The most revealing thing to me was Clinton getting up off his chair and walking to the very edge of the audience," he says. "He got as far into them as he could when he answered them. . . . The body language of that was very powerful as far as I was concerned."[25]

Another Clinton technique was to ask his questioners questions. This maximized his appearance of accessibility. In late October on ABC's "Good Morning America," a woman who said she was expecting her fourth child asked Clinton about his health care plan during a question-and-answer session in an East Rutherford, New Jersey, diner. Instead of cranking out his stock answer to one of the most frequently asked questions of the campaign, Clinton used the query as a chance to connect briefly with the woman—and, through her, the many voters who said health care was among their top concerns.

"Do you have health insurance?" Clinton asked. "What's the deductible?"

Clinton nodded gravely as the nervous woman explained that she had insurance but that it was expensive. Then he launched into a description of his health care plan that went on even after host Charlie Gibson broke for a commercial.[26]

Few politicians can rev up a crowd like Clinton—as he did when we interviewed him and his running mate in Ocala, Florida, during their October 1992 bus trip across that key state. Hundreds of Clinton and Gore supporters gathered around the buses to watch and cheer on their candidates. Clinton shook hands and talked with so many people that Tammy had to practically shove him into his seat so we could begin the show. I thought the Secret Service was going to shoot her. It was more like a rock concert than an interview, which was how Clinton liked it.

"You know," he confided as we were about to go on the air, "we're on hallowed ground."

"What do you mean?" I asked.

"Elvis played here," he said. He even knew the date!

Gore was not quite the talk-show natural Clinton was, but he'd had plenty of experience. He was a frequent guest of mine on TV and the radio—and a friend. I appreciated it, for instance, when he appeared on our show during the Democratic National Convention without his jacket and in suspenders—wardrobe à la King. And CNN anchor Shaw was envious. "I wish I could take my jacket off," he said when he interrupted our interview for a convention update.

"You can," I told him. "Go ahead, Bernie. Try it once."

"If you've got suspenders," Gore added.[27]

In interviews Gore often seems as if he is trying to hide how personable and funny he really is. That is a hard act for someone who is genuinely pleasant, so I think he does better in longer formats than he does when he's sound-biting on the evening news. I don't know if Gore believes that. If you ask, he'll laugh. "Stiff and wooden me?!" he says incredulously.[28]

A seductive caller from Asheville, North Carolina, drew out the sometimes awkward senator when she propositioned him on our show in September 1992. "I know I probably shouldn't say this," she said, "but I think you're a very handsome man. . . . Are you available for a date on Friday night?"

Gore's eyes popped open, and he laughed. He had no idea who was on the phone.

"No," I told the caller, "he's not available. He's happily married."

"Come on!" the woman said.

"That's the answer," Gore explained. "I'm not available."

"Not even for your wife?"

Gore looked completely baffled now. "Yes," he stammered, "for my wife."

The caller laughed. "Hi, this is Tipper," she said. "I'm calling you from Asheville. You're doing great."[29]

What a look on Gore's face! Here he was on live television, and the poor guy hadn't recognized his own wife's voice. Tipper Gore will have that on her husband forever. She even has a photograph of his expression at that moment, which the vice president says is "hanging prominently" in their house.[30]

Unlike Gore, Democratic primary challenger Jerry Brown was better at sound bites than he was in longer interviews. No matter what you would ask, the problem—as the former California governor and state party chairman saw it—was a corrupt political system of Washington insiders, egged on by the Establishment media and fed with funds from special interests and political action committees. Oh, and call our 800 number and please make a one hundred dollar donation. He was like a tape recorder—or a television evangelist.

Brown knew the part of a dark-horse presidential contender well, having played it in 1976 and 1980. His talk about the potential of satellite technology during those races earned him the nickname "Governor Moonbeam"—and his musings on spiritual matters after that made it stick. But, ironically, technology did a lot for

Brown's campaign in 1992. He was, for example, the first presidential candidate to hold a national town meeting on a commercial
computer network, answering typed-in questions from Compu-
Serve subscribers around the country on education, trade, health
care, and extraterrestials.

"Governor Brown," one computer user asked, "would you
support the release of supposed secret U.S. [documents] concern-
ing UFOs?"

"Yes," Brown answered from his own terminal, "but where
are they?"[31]

Brown introduced the toll-free telephone number to presidential politics long before Ross Perot had such success with his 800
number. Brown first mentioned his campaign's free phone line on
my radio show in fall of 1991, and he plugged it continually from
then on—in interviews, speeches, debates, whatever the occasion.
It was his mantra. In fact, when he came on "Larry King Live" in
late March, a viewer called from Montreal to ask why he had not
given out the number yet. I was wondering, too. "We set a record
tonight," I said to Brown. "We went thirty-five minutes, almost,
and you never gave [the number]."[32]

A couple of weeks later Brown went on ABC's "Nightline" to
refute dubious charges that when he was governor he had hosted
parties at which guests used marijuana and cocaine. Brown flatly
denied these allegations in an interview with host Ted Koppel.

"We are totally out of time . . . ," Koppel said near the end
of the program. "Have you said everything you wanted to say on
this?"

"I want to say one more thing, Ted," Brown answered. "Please,
if you support me, call 1-800-462-1112. . . . If you think this is

the way the media ought to treat a candidate for president, okay. But if you think we ought to be fighting back, we the people, call, make those donations, and we'll keep going. We're never gonna stop."[33]

That's what a political consultant would call "sticking to your message." And as Perot showed with his anti-Washington campaign rhetoric, it was a message voters wanted to hear. When Tsongas dropped out of the Democratic race, Brown inherited the anti-Clinton vote—and even beat the Arkansas governor in Connecticut the day before Brown appeared on our show. At some point, though, Brown's routine got old. The public wanted more matter, less art. Clinton beat Brown in the crucial New York primary in early April. In the California primary in June, near the end of the process, Brown won only 19 percent of the vote. Governor Moonbeam was still a little too "spacey" for most voters.

President Bush also seemed to be in his own world for much of the early part of the 1992 campaign. And it didn't help that his garbled syntax and mind-numbing sentence structures made him sound confused and out of it sometimes. In this regard, he was never a great TV performer, as many of his top advisers will freely admit. "The president is someone who did not come up being a television person . . . ," says Robert M. Teeter, the Republican pollster who chaired Bush's reelection campaign. "He is of a generation that was not used to this, and he also had a little more formal view of the propriety of what you do as president and what you don't."[34]

Propriety aside, Bush and his advisers decided late in the campaign that talk shows were a good vehicle for trying to make the

president look accessible, in-touch. But by that point in the race—
and his presidency—TV appearances could do only so much to
change the widespread public perception that he was "out of touch,"
as a cranky caller from Tampa, Florida, put it when we interviewed Bush in early October. It was his second appearance on
our show that week. This time, we were on location at the Arneson
River Theater in San Antonio, Texas.

"I am not happy with you," the Tampa caller told the president. "For two years, you did not recognize that people were hurting out here and we were in a recession. I feel like you have not
come clean on Iran-Contra. And I'm tired of your party and you
preaching to us about family values."

Bush shrugged. "I'll put you down as 'doubtful,' fellow."

It was a funny comeback. But Bush's trouble was that a lot of
people were "doubtful." And I don't think he helped himself with
any of those people when he pooh-poohed the Clinton campaign's
popular bus tours. "I'm not going to do that," he said. "I'm president, and I don't think you need to take a bus tour to stay in
touch. I think you can stay in touch . . . a lot of ways." But Bush
had to prove it, and he didn't know how.

He also didn't help himself with his answer to my question
about Bill Clinton's week-long trip to Moscow when he was a
Rhodes Scholar studying at Oxford. Clinton had said he'd gone to
the Soviet Union simply as a tourist. But conservative Republicans in Congress—as well as members of Bush's own campaign
team—had been trying to make an issue of the visit by suggesting that there was some subversive motive behind it. They were
also encouraging reporters to pursue unsubstantiated rumors that
Clinton had considered relinquishing his citizenship while he

was involved with student protests in England against the Vietnam War.

"What do you make of the Clinton Moscow trip thing," I asked Bush, purposely trying to be as vague as possible with my question. Bush could have gone anywhere with his answer. He could have dismissed the issue, taken the high road. He didn't.

"Larry," he said, "I don't want to tell you what I really think, because I don't have the facts. . . . But to go to Moscow, one year after Russia crushed Czechoslovakia, not remember who you saw . . ." He trailed off, careful to appear not to make the charge everyone knew he was making anyway. "I'm just saying, level with the American people," he said, "on the draft, on whether he went to Moscow, how many demonstrations he led against his own country from a foreign soil. Level, tell us the truth, and let the voters then decide who to trust or not."[35]

I was surprised Bush was willing to personally go so far out on this issue, especially since all the charges about Clinton's activities were so unsubstantiated. Certainly there were voters who thought this was an important issue, but those voters probably were voting for Bush already. He wasn't winning anybody over. In fact, the criticism of him in the press over the next several days for resorting to McCarthyism may have lost him votes.

Then–White House spokesman Marlin Fitzwater says the Moscow trip and the protests were issues Bush felt strongly about, and he couldn't hide his feelings. "It was true and honest George Bush . . . ," Fitzwater says. "Obviously we would have been better off if he had left that part out, if he had not mentioned the Moscow part. He could have just said he didn't know anything about the details of it and left it hanging out there. But that's not the way he felt. The thing about George Bush was he was not programmable, and he was honest. . . . He said what he thought, and he told the truth, and that's the way he felt. There was no stopping him."[36]

Bush's "Joe McCarthy" routine overshadowed his "average-Joe" moments that night—which were probably more along the lines of what his aides hoped to get out of his appearance on our show. At one point a caller from Cleveland, Ohio, accused the president of claiming Texas as his home state to avoid paying income taxes in Maine, where the Bushes had a home. Bush's address in Texas was a Houston hotel room, but he and his wife did own property there, as the president explained. Bush said he was legal resident of Texas and that he had a Texas driver's license to prove it.

That seemed funny to me. He had been vice president for eight years and president for almost four. I imagined that the Secret Service chauffeured him around most of the time and didn't let him behind the wheel much. What would Bush need a license for? So I asked. "When was the last time you drove?"

Bush said he sometimes drove a truck in Maine and when he went hunting in Texas. He also said he had a car in Washington that he didn't get to drive too often. "I'll drive around . . . the oval in front of the White House," he said.

That was a pretty funny image to me, too. I imagined tourists at the gate of the White House watching the president doing laps in a Datsun.

"And still a Texas driver's license?" I asked.

"Still," Bush said. "You want to see it?"

"Yes," I said. What was I going to say?

CUE THE TALENT · 91

Bush pulled out his wallet and produced the card; there was a picture of one of his grandchildren in the slot behind it. I showed the license to the camera. "President George W. Bush," it said. I'd never seen a license that listed someone's title like that. "The White House, 1600 Pennsylvania Avenue. . . . 6'1". . . . Birthdate: 6/12/24. . . . Expiration date: 6/12/93." While his wallet was out, he showed us his American Express card, too—as he had at a photo opportunity once when a young boy challenged Bush to prove he was in fact the president. "George Bush, President of the United States," it said. The card expired in 1994.

"I'm legal, see?" Bush said as he took his license back. "Where's your car? Let's go for a drive."[37]

This was pretty light stuff, especially for a president who had resisted appearing on shows like ours because he did not want to "trivialize" or diminish his office. To me it was the same as Bush bringing out his dog, Millie, to sleep by our feet during an interview with him and the First Lady at the White House two days earlier. This was the president's way of reminding our audience that he was a real person, a likable person who drove and hunted and shopped and had a dog—just like them. Even someone as serious as ABC's David Brinkley would have looked at the president's driver's license if he offered.

Bush was not a bad guy. I don't think I know anyone who has met Bush and said they did not like him personally. But times were getting past him. Bush spent his career in public service preparing to be a Cold War leader. What could he do when, in his first term, communism collapsed in Europe, the Berlin Wall crumbled, and the Soviet Union ceased to exist? It was like *The Producers,* a film in which Mel Brooks's characters try to stage a bad Broadway show (about Hitler) as a tax write-off. Instead of bombing, though, the musical is a hit. "Where did I go right?" one of the producers asks. That's Bush.

Bush's running mate, Dan Quayle, was a frequent guest on our show and, in many ways, a better spokesman for the administration than the president. Quayle's two primary missions under Bush were to chair the president's Council on Competitiveness, through which he determined how many federal laws and regulations were enforced, and to raise funds for the Republican Party and GOP candidates. Both jobs kept him in close touch with the business community, from industrial leaders to small businesspeople. So he recognized and understood the economic anxiety in the country better—and sooner—than many others in the administration.

Talk shows were good forums for Quayle. Answering audience questions, Quayle showed he could talk knowledgeably about the economy, the deficit, job retraining—anything the public wanted to ask. He was completely different from the gaffable idiot our viewers and listeners saw lampooned in news reports, political cartoons, and on late-night television. Call-in programs were the perfect medium for a politician who had trouble getting the press to take him seriously.

"How do you get around the media?" asks the much-derided former vice president. "By using the media."[38]

Quayle also learned from his mistakes, as he demonstrated when we got into a conversation about homosexuality during a late-October interview. "If one of your children or somebody was gay . . . they're still part of the family," he said.

"Okay, you're with children again," I said. "So if one of your children were gay, you'd support them?"

Quayle laughed. "No, no, no, no . . . ," he said. "Hey, Larry, let me tell you something. I got into trouble one time answering a hypothetical question like that."[39]

It probably won't be the last time, either. But don't write off Dan Quayle too quickly. He'll be back.

We probably have not heard the last of Patrick J. Buchanan, either. Bush's opponent in the Republican primaries had a special advantage on television: that's how he makes his living. The former Nixon and Reagan aide cohosts CNN's "Crossfire." And, if elected, he would have been the first "pinch-hit host of 'Larry King Live' to become president of the United States," as I said when he was a guest on our show in February 1992—the day after his surprisingly strong showing in New Hampshire.[40] One night in 1989 I got terribly sick shortly before we went on the air. I was dizzy and could not even sit in my chair. Pat rushed in and took over for me while I went to the doctor. He has always been a terrific friend.

Since the election Buchanan has launched a new national radio talk show, on which he debates issues with his callers and a rotating series of liberal cohosts. I don't know if he will run for president again in 1996, but a show like that is a great way for a candidate to build a national following. As *Los Angeles Times* media critic Tom Rosenstiel points out in *Strange Bedfellows,* his book on the 1992 election, that is exactly what one of Buchanan's former White House bosses, Reagan, did with his nationally broadcast daily radio commentary after he left office as governor of California.[41]

Reagan, a former actor, perfected the television-age presidency. Certainly, no one has seemed more "presidential" on television than Reagan. Deaver remembers watching Reagan's whole body change as he passed through the French doors of the Oval Office. "I don't care what time of day it was," he says, but "when he passed the curtain his shoulders would go back and he'd walk as if the Rose Garden were filled with cameras. . . . The only other person I ever saw who was like that was the Queen of England. . . . I don't think she knew. It was just the life that they'd led. I mean their lives had been [spent] performing." [42]

Reagan's biggest problem if he had to campaign on a talk show now would be having to perform without a script. He was always at his best when his material was prepared. A week before George Bush left office, for instance, I went to the White House to see him award Reagan the Medal of Freedom. During the reception I spoke briefly with the former president. "I always liked sitting under Lincoln's picture," Reagan told me, pointing to a portrait of the Civil War president. "I don't know why." That's nice, I thought, and wandered off to get an orange. A little while later I heard him talking to someone else. "I always liked sitting under Lincoln's picture," he said. "I don't know why." This was small talk for him. During his prepared remarks, however, Reagan was in top form. His delivery and his timing were flawless. "What better time and place to thank this great country for its blessings on me than here today in America's house," he said. "This marks the two hundredth anniversary of the laying of the cornerstone of the White House. By the way, my back is still killing me." [43]

Reagan was so likable on television, but I wonder if our callers would have cut him to pieces if he had been a candidate in 1992. When he came on our show in January 1991 to plug his memoirs, a viewer in Los Angeles asked why his administration had not done anything to warn the American people about the multi-billion-dollar savings and loan disaster. "Because I didn't know what was going on there . . . ," Reagan answered. "There are, you know, so many agencies and departments and so forth of government, and you're dependent on these people to bring you up to date on something that's going on. Well, I was never notified of any great problem or trouble with the savings and loan."[44] Try that one on the voters now.

The gaffes and memory lapses he sometimes displayed during White House press conferences made Reagan someone people could relate to. But during our 1991 interview, one month before the former president's eightieth birthday, Reagan told me how frustrating those lapses could be to him. He said he would see people he knew and recognized from his administration—people whose jobs and responsibilities he could even remember—but he could not remember their names. It was the same with some of his films. "I've been surprised lately when I've looked at a movie that I made quite some time ago," he said. "And what really surprises me is, yes, I remember that movie and the whole story and everything, except there will come a scene on there in which I'm involved, and I'll find that I have no memory whatsoever of doing that particular scene." He laughed. "And it bothers me."[45]

Maybe Reagan would have been a great talk-show candidate. Come to think of it, he could have been a great talk-show host. He was a fine baseball announcer, once upon a time.

The wonderful thing about talk-show democracy is that it *is* a democracy, and any two viewers may turn off their television sets after an interview and have completely different impressions of a guest. But I do think we give them a good look at who our guests are. People are transparent when you put them in front of the cameras, which is why we use lots of close-ups. No one, not the most disciplined performer, can control every gesture, every expression, all the time—but those things all transmit important information to viewers. The problem is that the information is ambiguous. If a candidate licks his lips while he listens to a question, what does that mean? Is it a hard question, one he doesn't want to answer? Is he nervous? Is he lying? Dodging? Or should we have filled up his coffee mug during the commercial break?

Still, there are things you can learn about a person just from watching him or her that you would never learn from a newspaper account or a nightly news sound bite. They have nothing to do with content. They're not things you would find in transcripts or if you were listening with your eyes closed, like a radio show. But they are details you can see for yourself that suggest something about a candidate. They are the sort of judgments you might make about a person if you were introduced at a party or over dinner. No press analysis or campaign spin can affect these impressions. Viewers can only gauge such things individually, since anyone watching may read something completely different into a gesture, a smile, a frown, a nod, or even a sip.

"Most leaders are actors," Nixon has said. "People like to glamorize their leaders, and leaders tend to glamorize themselves. MacArthur with his riding crop and corncob pipe, Patton with his pearl-handled revolvers, Churchill with his strut, FDR with his jaunty cigarette holder—all were acting to an extent. In fairness, each man's public posture was only an extension of his private personality. They may not have done it consciously, but the effect was to create mystique of difference and dignity." [46]

Talk shows break down that mystique. They show us the

person behind the riding crop and the revolvers and the strut and the cigarette, the speech, the attack, the 800 number, and the sob stories. If a candidate spends enough time in front of the cameras, it doesn't matter what he or she says. The viewers will see the truth for themselves—eventually.

Danziger in The Christian Science Monitor © *1992 TCSPS.*

"It's Just That Simple"

THE THURSDAY BEFORE the election Ross Perot was our guest for a ninety-minute edition of "Larry King Live" at CNN in Washington. After the interview, as I was escorting Perot to his car downstairs, we ran into a large contingent of police officers. There had been a bomb threat, they told us, and Perot was the target. They were there to escort him to the airport.

Perot took the news of the bomb threat calmly. He had refused Secret Service protection during the campaign because he thought it would make him feel isolated. Sometimes he had a driver, occasionally he used his own security guards, but he preferred to drive himself and rarely traveled with an entourage. I had asked him why earlier that night on the show. "If I never stop for red lights, [if] I'm in motor cavalcades . . . [with] more policemen than a Third World funeral for a king in front of me, I don't know there's any problem in this world," he had said.[1]

Perot told the officers that his life had been threatened many times. He had led a long and productive life, he said, and had gotten more from this world than any reasonable person could ask for. They, on the other hand, were young men with young families, and he could not bear to put them in harm's way to protect himself. "So, gentlemen," he concluded, "go home."

The police officers seemed genuinely moved. Not only did I think they would trade their lives for his, but they would probably vote for him. I'm sure it was rare for them to meet anyone of any importance in Washington who turned down a police escort. "We're taking you to the airport," the officer in charge insisted.

Perot, never willing to concede a fight, then did what he does best. He negotiated. Okay, he said, they could escort him to the airport, but no sirens and only two unmarked police cars. Three police cars, the commanding officer countered, two marked and one unmarked. Deal. They agreed. But as they were leaving the studio, Perot told the police that he had to stop by the Vietnam War Memorial on his way back to his plane at National Airport. He liked to visit the memorial at night.

"Oh, shit," the commanding office said.

Meanwhile, I'm thinking, If there's a bomb in this building, I've got to get out of here.

As it turned out, there was no bomb and everyone got home safely. Looking back, though, I really got to see Perot in action that night: Perot the wheeler-dealer, Perot the statesman, Perot the veterans' advocate—even Perot the target of this plot or that. More people ask me about Perot than anyone I have ever interviewed.

He was a guest on "Larry King Live" nine times in 1991 and 1992, including the February '92 show on which he unofficially announced his candidacy. So people often think he and I have a special link, as if I alone understand the billionaire's thoughts and actions.

President Bush, a fellow Texan, had known Perot for more than twenty years, but even he thought I had some special insight. During a White House interview in early October, I asked Bush about Perot's motives for running. "I'll leave that to you, Larry," Bush said. "You're the Perot expert. . . . You're the living oracle on this man."

"I just ask him questions," I said, "like with you."

"Well, but you can judge," Bush said. "You're entitled to an opinion. You're pretty good about keeping it, I must say. . . . But someday . . . I'm going to deprogram you, and you [can] tell me what you think about [Perot], because you've been around him much more."[2]

Off the air that night, Bush tried again. "What does he have against me?" the president asked.

"You tell me," I said. "You've known him longer."

Perot and I did bond over a pair of cuff links the first time he was on the show, in January 1991. We were in Los Angeles, and I was going to an awards dinner as soon as we went off the air. During a commercial break early in the program, one of my cuff links broke. Perot had never met me before, but he generously lent me his, a gift from his wife, Margot, with his initials engraved on them. When we came out of the break, Perot was still helping me put them on.

That was the beginning of a beautiful friendship. But the truth of the matter is that Perot's frequent appearances on our show had more to do with my senior executive producer, Tammy, than it did with me. She spoke and joked frequently with Perot on the phone. Both are aggressive straight-shooters, so they hit it off right away. She would explain to him the advantages of appearing on our program, and he would tell her how to deal with the building contractors working on her home. Sharon Holman, Perot's spokeswoman, says her boss put up with me so he could talk to Tammy. "There's no question that behind every great man there's an even more powerful woman," Holman says.[3] Don't I know it.

Perot may have announced his candidacy on our show, but his motives for running were never entirely clear to me. He was certainly angry at the Bush and Reagan administrations for their handling of questions about Vietnam-era prisoners of war and soldiers still listed as missing in action—issues of great personal concern to him since his high-profile efforts to deliver Christmas presents to American POWs during the Vietnam War. But, more important, he shared the public's frustration with Washington for its failure to address the nation's economic problems. Growing deficits and declining economic competitiveness were his top concerns. Perot thought Congress and the federal government needed someone with business acumen, an independent mediator, who could make reform digestible—or, if necessary, ram it down their throats.

That's what he had done as head of a gubernatorial task force on education in Texas in the mid-1980s. There Perot had milked new spending for schools from a resistant legislature and helped pass a controversial "no pass, no play" rule requiring students to get good grades before they could play high school football—the state religion in Texas. If he could beat high school coaches in his home state, Perot thought, he could beat the political consultants, bureaucrats, and foreign lobbyists who were fouling things up in the nation's capital.

Was it an ego thing? Of course it was. But Perot wasn't any more egotistical than Bush, Clinton, or anyone else who has sought that office. Anyone who thinks he or she should live in the White House has to have a lot of ego—and more than a little chutzpah. But I don't think Perot anticipated the response that would be generated by his offer to run for president. In fact, Perot actually thought he had smothered any enthusiasm about his possible candidacy by challenging those who were encouraging him to run to figure out complicated state election laws on their own and put his name on the ballot in all fifty states as an independent. "I expect everybody to go very silent at this point, Larry . . . ," Perot said that night in February. "That puts it to bed."[4]

I wasn't sure myself what to expect from Perot's challenge. I knew many voters were not happy with their choices for president, Democrat or Republican. The idea of an attractive alternative riding in on a white horse would certainly have a lot of appeal. But I didn't know if they were actually willing to pull the lever for a "none of the above" candidate. After all, no third-party or independent candidate had ever been elected president. The last serious independent challenge had been in 1980, when Republican primary candidate John B. Anderson, a former Illinois congressman, dropped out of the race to run as an independent against Ronald Reagan and Jimmy Carter. Anderson won more than five million votes, less than 7 percent of the total. In 1968 independent candidate George C. Wallace received ten million votes, 13.5 percent of the total. That was a lot in a year when Republican Richard

Nixon beat Vice President Hubert Humphrey by just over 510,000 votes. But the Alabama governor was a regional candidate. He carried six states in the South, winning forty-six votes in the electoral college, the actual system by which we chose our presidents. But that was less than a fifth of the electoral vote Wallace would have needed to win. I didn't know if Perot could win either, but—like Wallace—I thought he might change the election year math for the two major-party candidates.

In the beginning most journalists didn't give Perot even that much credit. The press virtually ignored his offer to run. The *Los Angeles Times* mentioned Perot's announcement in an anonymous, 130-word blurb two days after his appearance on our show.[5] The *New York Times* discussed Perot's possible candidacy two weeks later in a page eleven story by Doron P. Levin, a former *Wall Street Journal* reporter who wrote a book about Perot in 1989.[6] Otherwise, the enthusiasm Perot's announcement generated around the country went unnoticed by reporters outside of Texas until mid-March.[7]

Washington's political press was especially oblivious to Perot's potential, as I discovered in early April at columnist George Will's annual party to celebrate the opening of the baseball season. I talked about Perot's chances with Sam Donaldson and our host. Both had tangled with Perot during an unusually cantankerous interview on ABC's "This Week with David Brinkley" two weeks before.[8] They were unimpressed and dismissive. "Come on, Larry," Donaldson said. "It's a one-day story." Their feelings were typical—in Washington.

The earliest Beltway sage whom I remember taking Perot seriously was commentator David Gergen. He was one of the first people to call our offices at CNN for a transcript of Perot's February appearance. Then he flew to Dallas to interview Perot over dinner at the businessman's home. The populist billionaire "could turn the race upside down—and maybe America, too," Gergen wrote in *U.S. News & World Report* two weeks after Perot was on our show. "His kind of leadership has a powerful appeal, for reasons that have less to do with H. Ross Perot than with the sorry state of American politics."[9] By the time Gergen wrote his column in early March, Perot's supporters had already collected enough signatures to put their candidate on the ballot in Tennessee, and petition committees were up and running in most other states.

Perot was as surprised as many in the press by the enthusiasm his potential candidacy produced. "It never occurred to me that it would create the reaction that it did," he says.[10] But the businessman quickly recognized the power that talk television and its huge audiences gave him over conventional campaigners—and conventional campaign reporters. The reaction to his announcement on "Larry King Live," and the continuing reaction every time he came back or appeared on "Donahue" or my radio show and other programs, showed him that he did not need big rallies and photo opportunities to reach the voters.

"If you speak to a thousand people a night seven nights a week," Perot says, "it takes you about three years to talk to a million [people]. So on shows where you get twenty and thirty million people, some of these huge shows, you realize the multiplier effect [you] can create just with one short comment like that— a nationwide reaction. And that's the power of television that does not exist in any other medium."[11]

So Perot was always accessible to us, unlike some of our guests, who often can take weeks of staff work to book on the show. Once during the campaign, Perot was on a boat in Annapolis for a campaign event. While he was within driving distance, we thought we would ask if he wanted to come on the show that night. So his Dallas headquarters transferred producer Tom Farmer's call directly to Holman, who was with Perot on the boat with a cellular phone.

"Hey, Ross!" Farmer heard Holman shout. "Do you want to do 'Larry King' tonight?"

"Sure," Perot answered.

It was just that simple.

As John Sununu puts it, Perot saw campaigning as a sales problem, and television was a way to reach the customer: "The encyclopedia salesman theory is that if the guy gets into five homes, he's going to sell one. And Ross Perot wanted to get into as many homes as he could. . . . Ross Perot is a wonderful encyclopedia salesman." [12]

Perot's folksy manner was perfect for television—especially interactive television with live audiences or phone calls. In June Perot dazzled callers and viewers on NBC's "Today" show with some of the best of his dizzying common sense, charm, and mixed metaphors. This was the tape Dana Carvey must have studied to master his imitation for "Saturday Night Live."

Perot on balancing the budget:

"Now, if you can't stand a little pain, and you can't stand a little sacrifice, and you can't stand to trip across the desert with limited water, we're never going to straighten this country out. So if you like Lawrence Welk music, I'm not your man."

On debates:

"I would not have any interest at all in one of those, you know, blow-dried guys sitting there asking all three of us questions in a pompous way."

On public opinion polls:

"These are just kind of like the speedometer on your car. You may be doing sixty, you may be doing thirty. And so it's goofy stuff for me."

On health care:

"We are buying a front-row box seat, and we're not even getting to see a bad show from the bleachers."

On gun control:

"When I grew up, we all had guns, but we didn't shoot one another."

I thought Willard Scott might have out-Rossed Perot when the popular weatherman asked him a question. "If you get to the White House," Scott said, "is it going to be all-bean chili, or beef and beans, or all beef?"

Perot hardly stuttered. "Well, it will be whatever my wife puts on the table," he said. "And we will have broccoli, I can assure you."

This "anticandidate" from Texarkana, Texas, wasn't always decipherable, but he was usually entertaining. And, for someone with a net worth of more than three billion dollars, he was as good as Clinton at reminding people of his humble origins. He was the candidate who broke his nose breaking horses, who delivered newspapers as a boy on horseback. His father was a successful cotton agent, so when a "Today" show viewer from Cross Plains, Indiana, called to ask about the dairy industry, Perot slipped comfortably into his rhetorical overalls. "That is a beautiful question . . . ," he said. "See, I grew up in a farming environment, and any time it rains, I think about the farmers. When it's a slow rain with the water going into the ground, I still think about that. When it rains too much, I worry about the seed rotting."

Later in the show, a caller phoned in a question from Alexandria, Louisiana. "I've spent time in Alexandria," Perot said. "I hitchhiked down there when I was a boy to visit my aunt." [13] People could imagine Perot as a young man hitchhiking in Louisiana, and they liked that about him. They could even imagine him doing it now. Perot might have been rich, but he wasn't country club, he wasn't limousine. He wasn't above people. He was like them.

"Today" producer Jeff Zucker knew entertainment when he saw it and decided on the spot to keep Perot on the air with co-host Katie Couric for the program's full two hours. Perot took questions from twenty-one callers that morning in June—and the ratings were terrific. "That's what politics is," Zucker says. "It's somewhere between news and entertainment." [14]

Perot was rating as well with voters as he was with the network ratings watchers. By early June, in fact, he was creeping into the lead in many polls. A Times Mirror Center survey put his support at 36 percent, five points ahead of Bush. That was a first for an independent challenger facing an incumbent president. Clinton was in third place with 27 percent. [15] The Arkansas governor nailed down the Democratic nomination in the California primary on June 2, but exit polls in that key state showed Perot trouncing him there with the support of 41 percent of the primary voters; Clinton had 27 percent and Bush had 23. Winning California in the fall would give Perot fifty-four electoral votes, more than Wallace had won in six states in 1968. And Perot was doing as well in many other states, too. In a little more than three months, Perot had scrambled all the election projections. And he hadn't even formally declared that he would run yet.

The day after the California primary, the unofficial candidate hired two top political strategists to run his undeclared campaign—Republican Ed Rollins and Democrat Hamilton Jordan. Rollins had managed Ronald Reagan's reelection campaign in 1984. Jordan had run Carter's campaigns in 1976 and 1980. Perot had promised his supporters the best campaign his money could buy and he seemed to be delivering. Having two well-respected politicos on his pay roll—along with the latest poll numbers—gave Perot's candidacy overnight legitimacy with the insiders. But taking the lead meant taking the hits.

Perot's advantage up to that point was that he was relatively unknown. The public was not holding him responsible for the recession. And he hadn't been ensnared in controversies over Gennifer Flowers or his draft record. With the primaries behind them, Perot's opponents and the press could turn their attention to him. Perot said he wanted to cut federal spending, but how much of his money came from federal contracts? Had he lobbied for special tax breaks? Did he use private investigators to harass business rivals? And what about his connections to fringe groups involved in MIA and POW issues? Was he thin-skinned? Dictatorial? These were among the questions raised in news stories and by his opponents as Perot's candidacy gained momentum that spring.

Clinton told our viewers that Perot was "the moment's rage," someone who "sounds great" but had no real plan.[16] Vice President Dan Quayle went further, calling Perot "a temperamental tycoon who has contempt for the Constitution of the United States."[17]

Press probing brought out an unattractive side of Perot. His exchanges with reporters were often tense and defensive. He was a completely different person with journalists than he was answering viewer questions on call-in programs. He exploded, for instance, in a May 1992 interview with Linda Wertheimer of National Public Radio when she asked him if his lobbying on behalf of his business interests in Washington squared with his anti-Washington political rhetoric. This was a "classic setup," Perot said. "I assume this is the sole reason for your taped interview. . . . Whoever you're trying to do a favor for, you've done it, and I'm sure you had a smirk on your mouth as you got me into this."

Wertheimer tried to ask Perot if his business practices would be as difficult to explain in a campaign as other candidates' "personal behavior."

"I'm not going to worry about it for a minute," he said, "and I just assume that there will be days when people like you show up, doing a favor for somebody, and you've done it." [18]

Perot was not quite so defensive when I pressed him on these and other matters in late June, but news stories about him and criticism—especially from the White House and the Republican party—clearly were getting to him. He accused his critics of engaging in "character assassination and personality distortion."

But wasn't his background fair game? I asked.

"My *true* background is fair game," he said. But his opponents were painting a picture of him that had "nothing to do with anything except fiction."

"How about the thoughts that you are thin-skinned?" I asked.

"Look at everything that's been written about me over the years," he said. "See, I became autocratic and thin-skinned right after [the campaign] started. This is what is called redefining your opponent's character. . . . Everybody said that when it got rough I couldn't take it, right? Well, I think it's pretty rough now, and I'm not sitting here trembling with my teeth chattering, scared to death."

Later in the show GOP Chairman Rich Bond phoned in to accuse Perot of making "very wild and unsubstantiated charges about dirty tricks by the Republican Party." Bond said Perot's claims were "fantasy" and asked him to produce "one shred of evidence."

"You're telling me you don't have a huge number of people in opposition research?" Perot said. "You're telling me you don't have a huge number of people going through every shred of evidence they can find about anything relating to me? . . . That's what you're telling the American people, Rich?"

Bond insisted that "repeating your own words back to you" was not a dirty trick.

Perot said GOP operatives often "boasted" about their exploits against him, "and half the people they boast to call me." Perot also said Bond's staff called reporters to pass along information about him. "And on any given day, I'll have six reporters call me . . . five minutes after you send them the message of the day. Half of them will call laughing, saying this is from your dirty tricks department."

Bond scoffed. "This is just fantasyland, Larry," he said.[19]

I do not doubt that Perot had many enemies in business and politics who were happy to share information they had about him with the press and his campaign rivals. And some of the questions they raised about him were legitimate issues. Perot did not understand the obsession with his background and character, but he had made those issues relevant by making himself the central issue of his undeclared campaign. He hadn't released a specific economic program yet, but according to Perot the specifics didn't matter. "There are wonderful plans on paper that can solve every problem . . . ," he said during a town meeting with ABC's Peter Jennings in late June. But "ideas are worthless unless you implement them and execute them."[20]

Perot thought America needed to hire a contractor, a can-do businessman, who could turn those "blueprints" into "houses." But if he was offering himself as that sort of businessman, the public wanted to know what sort of businessman he was. People understood what it took to succeed in the private sector as he had. That was why he was rarely asked about his business practices when he was a private citizen—and why his press coverage had been much more positive before he became a presidential candidate. But many people were nervous about giving the powers of the nation's highest public office to someone who was used to operating behind the scenes. News stories suggesting he hired detectives to gather information about President Bush's family and finances or to keep track of his own children made people nervous.

Perot was also frustrated by all the questions he was asked about issues that he didn't think were important. He wanted to talk about the economy and the deficit, and that was it. Any other question was a distraction. "We love to concentrate on the nonmajor issues," he said, when "Today's" Katie Couric asked him if he thought views on abortion rights should be a litmus test for Supreme Court nominees.[21] On ABC's town meeting, the audience asked Perot questions about abortion and gay rights. "I'm not sure . . . we can stay preoccupied full-time with issues like this and solve the core problems that face our country," he said.[22] Maybe Perot was right. Maybe these issues are not as important as solving the nation's economic problems. But they are important issues to many people, as the fierce debate over President Clinton's plan to lift the ban on gays in the military showed in the early months of his administration.

As I considered Perot's troubles, I found myself thinking back to a remark Perot made on the show in February, when he first said he was willing to run. Earlier in the show, however, Perot insisted he had no interest in politics. "I wouldn't be temperamentally fit for it," he said—a quote Democrats and Republicans would later try to use against him.[23] I was beginning to wonder if Perot had been right. So, when he was on the show in June, I asked him what he had meant.

"I like to get things done," he said, "not just talk about things."

And that made him "temperamentally" unfit to run?

"Except," Perot said, "the thing I missed is the American people are tired of gridlock. They're tired of talk. They're tired of the president and the Congress throwing rocks at one another every day. And they want action. . . . The thing I thought might be a problem is an attraction."[24]

The attraction was wearing thin, however. And Perot was growing weary of the process. Three weeks after that interview, I was in New York for the Democratic National Convention. News rarely happens at conventions any more. On July 16 the exciting question du jour was how long Clinton's acceptance speech would be. His hour-long nominating speech for Michael Dukakis in Atlanta four years earlier had been so dull the only applause line began, "In conclusion." As it turned out the real news that day occurred long before Clinton stepped to the podium at Madison Square Garden. Halfway across the country, at a news conference in Dallas, Perot announced that he would not be a candidate for president after all. At that point his name was already on the ballot in about half the states.

Perot said he was concerned that no candidate would win a majority in the electoral college in a three-way race, throwing the election to the Democratic Congress to decide, and that would be "disruptive." He didn't want to provoke a constitutional crisis. "The Democratic party has revitalized itself," Perot said in Dallas. "They've done a brilliant job, in my opinion, in coming back. And I am hopeful that both parties will really focus on what the people are concerned about in this country."[25]

That was it? The man who had promised to shake up Washington didn't want to be "disruptive"? I knew there had to be more to it than that. The next night Perot flew to New York to explain himself on "Larry King Live," and we were flooded with calls for ninety minutes from angry and upset supporters. A caller from New York said Perot had treated the campaign "as a rich man's toy," playing with "the hopes and dreams of millions of Americans only to dash their hopes when it wasn't fun . . . anymore."

Cher called from Los Angeles to tell Perot that she would give up everything she was doing to volunteer for him, "as long as I know that, if I got into it . . . you wouldn't quit. . . . Whether you like it or not, you have to be there . . . ," Cher said. "Every infant movement needs a father. And you have to be it, whether you like it or not."

Cher's call surprised him, but Perot was visibly upset after a call from Cleveland. "The tears have just not stopped," the caller said. "We had a headquarters in Garfield Heights, Ohio, . . . and it was wonderful and refreshing to meet so many people from different areas who just drove by and would stop in because they supported you and loved you, Ross. Love for our country, yes, but knowing how much we loved you as a person was just as important to us. . . . You showed us honesty, love, and you truly wanted to change our country. Please, Ross, show us how much you care for us. Do what we went out to do for you."

Perot was deeply moved. "Well, I do care for you," he said, "and I love you. And I will remember for the rest of my life everything you just said. I know that I speak for you and everyone else when I say our objective is the country. The fact that you have those feelings for me personally means a great deal to me. I am incidental in the big picture. Getting the system to work is all important."[26]

A half hour more of this, and Perot probably would have reentered the race. But I also knew a part of him had never wanted to run—as he had said over and over the night he announced on our show in February. I wondered if he had been looking for an out since then. "Between now and the conventions we'll get both parties' heads straight . . . ," he had said at that time. "I think I can promise you a world-class candidate on each side. . . . By the conventions, you might say, 'Cripes, you know, it's all taken care of.' "[27] Had this been Perot's plan all along?

Perot's explanations for not running were not convincing. He insisted that gridlock and "partisan politics" would have prevented him from solving the nation's economic problems, even if he had won. People in Washington were obsessed with beating up on their opponents for political gain instead of fixing things, he said. "It's like being inside a washing machine while you're trying to do something very fragile."

But he knew that all along. Why, all of a sudden, couldn't he be an "effective president"? I asked. What had changed?

"I could be an effective president," he said, "If we didn't have this partisan stress."

"But you didn't know that in February?"

"I didn't appreciate it to the degree I do now."

"And what made you appreciate it?" I asked.

"Just being inside the tent," he said, "watching it. I didn't realize how vicious it was, how petty it was. . . . And, Larry, you just can't get anything done in that environment."

Our viewers were as skeptical as I was. "You're all dough and no show," said a caller from Jefferson City, Missouri—the "show-me" state. "Who got to you? I have a feeling somebody on the Republican side—the dirty tricksters—got to you. And you're not normally a man who's scared, but those people have scared me for the last twelve years and beyond that. And I just think somebody got to you, and I think they're making you drop out."

I had the same question. "Do you think [your opponents] tried to destroy you?" I asked.

"Larry, I refuse to make it personal . . . ," Perot said. "You know how the game is played. The average citizen out there knows how the game is played. . . . Boxing has the Marquis of Queensberry rules. You didn't hit below the belt, right? . . . This is mud wrestling with no rules; just anything goes, and, if one candidate can destroy the other, he will win by default."[28]

I didn't know how close we had come to discovering Perot's real reason for dropping out until much later. But on the set, after the show, Perot spoke privately with CNN president Tom Johnson. Johnson had worked in Dallas for many years. He and Perot were friends. Off the record Perot told Johnson that he had uncovered a Republican plot to disrupt his daughter's wedding that summer by circulating a picture of a lesbian scene with her face doctored in. "I was there, and he basically decided to open up quite candidly on some of this, and there were some very, very sensitive, personal aspects to it . . . ," Johnson recalls. "I think it was an intensely personal experience, and it was an intensely personal decision" to drop out.

Perot's off-the-record information put Johnson in a tough spot journalistically. If Perot thought the GOP or the Bush campaign had hatched such a plot, it would be a big scoop for CNN. But Johnson had given his word that he wouldn't use the story. "I guess you learn in this business that you . . . build a reputation for trust," he says. "And also there are ways that you can try to direct and guide your coverage based on that information without really breaking [your] word. I mean we did not go with a lot of the other speculation which other media people did about why he [dropped out] . . . that clearly was not well founded."[29]

Most of the rest of the country did not hear the story about Perot's daughter until later in the campaign, when "60 Minutes" asked Perot about it. Meanwhile, he is still grateful to Johnson for keeping their conversation off the record, despite its obvious news value. "He is a gentleman, and he honored it," Perot says.[30]

Perot also raised the matter with Bush when the president called to ask for his support. Bush said he would check on it, but Perot said he never heard back. Officials from the Republican party and the Bush campaign later denied that they had any plans to disrupt his daughter's wedding. Barbara Bush even told Perot so personally at one of the presidential debates in the fall. Perot has said he takes them at their word.

And whether the information about his daughter's wedding was true or not, Perot says he has no regrets over his decision to withdraw from the race. "I had to do what I had to do . . . ," he says. "That had everything to do with my daughter, and I don't care what anybody thinks about it. She is more important to me than all this other stuff, and you only get married once."[31]

Perot's anger over Republican dirty tricks even extended to Rollins, one of his own campaign managers. "I think he really got paranoid about the Republicans," Rollins says. "And I think he was always suspicious of my ties to the Republicans."

Rollins and Jordan had not been able to get Perot to agree on a campaign strategy. Rollins commissioned a poll to show Perot that Gulf War hero Norman Schwarzkopf did almost as well against Bush and Clinton as he did. His support had more to do with his opponents' faults than his strengths. To turn that protest vote into a winning majority, Rollins told Perot, he would have to campaign—travel, speak, advertise. "He didn't want to do anything until October," Rollins says. "I mean he believed his polls. He was a novice in the game of politics."

Rollins wanted Perot to start advertising in July "to define [and] build a movement, to make people feel this [was] not some crazy [thing]." Many "prominent Americans, very key Republicans and Democrats and business leaders," were willing to lend their name to Perot's campaign. But Perot "didn't see the need to advertise when he could go on the 'Today' show," Rollins says. "If he wanted to, he could have been president. . . . If he would have run a campaign and stayed in the race, certainly he and Bill Clinton would have fought for the presidency."

What was Perot's appeal? "Here's Mr. Can-Do," Rollins says, "someone [from] outside the system. He sure as hell isn't doing it for the power or the money. He's got all that. . . . Ego certainly is another factor, but of the three motivators, people would rather have ego drive [a candidate] than the other two."[32]

Shortly before Perot withdrew from the race, Rollins quit. Creative differences.

I'm sure Perot would dismiss any of Rollins's observations about him and his campaign, as he did in Dallas when I mentioned the Republican strategist during an interview in late September. "I probably didn't spend two hours with Mr. Rollins the whole time he was here," Perot said. "Some of my associates felt they needed advice from a person with his background. I humored them and let them bring him to Dallas, and the rest is history."

I asked Perot to respond to something Rollins had said about him on television earlier in the day. "It's ludicrous to even put him on television . . . ," Perot said. "This is a man who now makes a living pretending to know a great deal about me, who knows next to nothing about me because I had almost no contact with him. . . . That's the way the worm turns, though."[33]

On NBC's "Today" three months earlier, however, Perot had said Rollins was "incredibly gifted and talented." "Every day I work with Ed, it just gets to be more fun," he said. "He comes in, argues with me, raises Cain. See, I thrive on that. Now apparently, these are the kind of traits in his personality that created problems in some of his other ventures. . . . [But] I want someone to come in, kick over the chairs. . . . We have raging debate."[34]

I'm often asked if Perot is paranoid, as Rollins has suggested. Sure, as paranoid as anyone with three billion dollars. Hardly anyone walks up to Perot who doesn't want something, so he is naturally suspicious. Was he crazy? No more than any entrepreneur. You have to be able to see the world in a different way to leave a lucrative job at IBM to start a company that most everyone says will fail.

The person I know who is most like Perot is CNN founder Ted Turner. News audiences for the broadcast networks were shrinking when he created our twenty-four-hour-a-day news network. Few gave his enterprise much—if any—chance to succeed. Today he is one of the most influential broadcasters in the world. Entrepreneurs like Turner and Perot take chances. They think big, which is why the public is so drawn to them. When they succeed, they are visionaries. But when they fail, they look foolish—crazy. The 1992 election wasn't so clear cut. Perot was not elected president, but he was hardly a failure, which is why people have such mixed impressions of him.

The businessman candidate kept his nationwide army of volunteer "Perotistas" organized over the summer. By the end of September his name was on the ballot in all fifty states. Perot had also released his economic program, a paperback plan for cutting the deficit and fixing the economy. Budget experts were impressed by its seriousness and it quickly went to the best-seller list. These were the specifics he had needed the previous spring.

In late September Perot called his state coordinators together for a meeting in Dallas to decide if they should throw their support behind one candidate or the other or if Perot should reenter the race. Bush and Clinton both sent high-level delegations to the meeting to try to woo the billionaire and his supporters. Both camps had nice things to say about Perot's plan. "It seems . . . that's the one thing the two campaigns agree upon," a reporter said at a news conference that afternoon.

"I've been telling you guys for months," Perot said. "To know me is to love me."[35]

We flew down to Dallas that day, too, and put Perot on the show to get his reaction to the Bush and Clinton presentations—and to see what Perot's plans were. He was already talking like a candidate again. But he said it was up to his volunteers to decide. A caller from Atlanta wanted to know if he could take the heat. "It didn't seem like you were able to last time," the caller said, "so you got out of the kitchen."

Perot said he could handle anything his opponents or the press could throw at him, but he refused to spend any more time addressing issues that were not "critical to the future of this country." "Let everybody play 'gotcha' . . . ," he said. "Let everybody have fun at my expense."[36]

A few days later, Perot officially reentered the race. It was October already. Now Perot could run the intense, one-month campaign he had told Rollins he had always favored.

To sell his new economic plan, Perot supplemented the "free media" he got from "Larry King Live" and other shows with half-hour "infomercials," which he paid to air on broadcast television. "It's cost effective . . . ," the businessman explained to me in late October. "On even a big night the cost of three one-minute

commercials is about the same as thirty minutes."[37] And the ratings were astounding. Millions of Americans tuned in to watch
Perot sit behind a desk, flip through hand-held charts, and explain
his economic program.

The charts were a brilliant touch, too, straight out of *USA
Today*—the nation's most-looked-at newspaper. What a way to sell
and explain complicated ideas! Perot's opponents immediately recognized the power of Perot's bar graphs, pie charts, and fever lines
and seized on the idea. When Vice President Quayle appeared on
"Larry King Live" one week before the election, he came with a
chart to explain that the economy was growing faster than the
media had portrayed. Clinton appeared on the show the following
night with two counter graphs showing that the growth Quayle
had talked about hadn't amounted to much per person.[38] So I was
stunned the night after that when Perot appeared on our program
with no charts at all. "I sold them to Clinton and Quayle," the
expert salesman explained.[39]

Since the election Perot-like charts have become a regular part
of the nation's political dialogue. Hardly a political guest, including President Clinton, appears without some sort of graph any more.
Clinton even uses them in White House news conferences and
Oval Office speeches. And I won't be surprised the night Arnold
Schwarzenegger comes on the show with a chart to explain that,
due to foreign sales, his last film wasn't really a flop. Trust me; it's
only a matter of time.

Perot didn't bring his charts to the first presidential debate on
October 11, but he stole the show without them. Near the beginning of the evening, moderator Jim Lehrer asked the candidates
what distinguished them from their opponents. Bush and Clinton
said experience. "Well, they've got a point," Perot said. "I don't

have any experience in running up a four trillion dollar debt. I don't have any experience in gridlock government, where nobody takes any responsibility for anything and everybody blames everybody else. I don't have any experience in creating the worst public school system in the industrialized world, the most violent, crime-ridden society in the industrialized world. But I do have a lot of experience in getting things done. . . . I've got a lot of experience in not taking ten years to solve a ten-minute problem. So if it's time for action, I think I have the experience that counts. If there's more time for gridlock and talk and finger-pointing, I'm the wrong man."[40] The whole debate was vintage Perot. In the instant analysis afterward, he was declared the winner. Perot was back in the running.

But any momentum Perot might have gained that night was lost several days later after his running mate's performance at the vice presidential debate in Atlanta. Retired Vice Admiral James Stockdale, a decorated war hero who was tortured for eight years in a prison camp in North Vietnam, was never supposed to be Perot's real number two. Supporters in twenty-seven states needed to list a running mate on their petitions in order for Perot to qualify for the ballot. Stockdale, a longtime friend of Perot's, agreed in March to serve as the businessman's interim vice presidential candidate until he could choose his actual running mate. He never wanted to be on the ticket in the fall. On "Larry King Live" in March, my sometime stand-in, Bob Beckel, asked Stockdale if he would run as Perot's vice president in the fall if Perot wanted him to. "I don't want to talk about that because that's not part of our deal . . . ," Stockdale said. "I don't . . . have my heart set on it, and there's been no reason to believe that that was part of the deal, and I'm not secretly seeking anything."[41]

When Perot withdrew as a candidate in July, Rollins says the independent candidate's campaign had only seriously approached one potential vice presidential contender, Elizabeth Dole, Bush's former labor secretary. She expressed no interest.[42] By the time Perot reentered the race in early October, it was too late to switch horses. The admiral became Perot's running mate by default.

Stockdale could wax poetic explaining his running mate's virtues, but he was not well prepared to explain Perot's plans for governing, as he showed at the vice presidential debate. "Who am I? Why am I here?" he asked at the beginning of his introductory remarks.[43] Much of America was asking the same question.

If Perot could have switched running mates, Chrysler Chairman Lee Iacocca would have made a terrific vice presidential candidate. Two years before Perot launched his independent campaign for president, he and Iacocca had discussed starting a new political party. "We had breakfast one day" in Dallas, Perot recalls, "and he said I'm not sure that these two parties will ever be responsive to the people again, and maybe what we have to have is a third party. And we kicked that around." But Perot says he never thought to ask Iacocca to run with him in 1992. "I would have felt presumptuous going to Lee Iacocca saying, 'Would you be willing to run as vice president . . . ,' " he says. "You put the two of us together, and I'd say probably Lee ought to be at the top of the ticket and I ought to be the vice president."[44]

I suspect Iacocca would have said yes, and that would have been a formidable ticket. Iacocca described the same meeting with Perot during interviews with me later in 1992, and nothing he said then has changed my mind.

If seems to be the key word in discussing Perot's candidacy. If he had a different running mate. . . . If he had put his platform together sooner. . . . If he hadn't dropped out of the race. . . . If a lot of things, Perot could have been president. In fact, he still could someday. Perot maintains his flock as spiritual leader of "United We Stand America," a national organization that grew out of his campaign committee. And, at this writing, Perot could be a serious presidential challenger, either as an independent or as a Republican.

As it was, Perot spent about sixty million dollars of his own money and won 19 percent of the vote in 1992—more than any third-party or independent candidate since Theodore Roosevelt. As a "Bull Moose" candidate in 1912, Roosevelt won 27.4 percent of the vote—and he was a former president. The only other third-party candidate to do better than Perot was also a former president, Millard Fillmore, who won 21.5 percent of the vote when he ran as the Whig-American candidate in 1856. If Perot does not run for president again in 1996, he may only be a historical footnote, but he'll be a big one.

Not that I think his place in history matters a whole lot to Perot. There he is on "Larry King Live," "Today," "Meet the Press," charts in hand, ready to take on the president's economic program, the North American Free Trade Agreement, and so on. But I suspect the entrepreneur is as ambivalent as ever about his high profile in a political system he truly loathes. He likes rallies and town meetings and interacting with his volunteers. But he hates having his motives questioned. He is not "temperamentally" fit for it and would enjoy being a more-or-less anonymous billionaire again who could do what he liked and what he thought was right without his every action being scrutinized and assessed.

The day after the election Perot called me at home in Arlington,

Virginia. "I have a favor to ask you" he said. "There's a very elderly lady from Arkansas who is a huge fan of yours. It's her birthday, and she lives alone, and she's way up there in years, and she's not well." She was not a friend, he said, or a family member. She was just someone he met while visiting someone else he knew at the hospital. "Could you call her?"

It's hard to say no to a salesman like Ross Perot.

"SORRY, MIKE WALLACE, WE HAVE TO PUT YOU ON HOLD!...WE'VE GOT *DAN RATHER,*
BARBARA WALTERS, TOM BROKAW AND *TED KOPPEL* ON CALL-WAITING, BUT FIRST
A FAX FROM *KATIE COURIC* AND A FOLLOW-UP FAX FROM *PETER JENNINGS!...* "

By permission of Doug Marlette and Creators Syndicate.

Hot Air

TELEVISION PEOPLE OFTEN have a look: Edward R. Murrow had his cigarettes; David Letterman sports double-breasted jackets; Dan Rather tried sweaters.

For about five years now I've gone to work almost every night in shirtsleeves, a tie, and a pair of my trademark suspenders. My ex-wife Sharon first suggested I try the "braces." Suspenders would look good on me, she promised. So I went out and bought a pair. That night several viewers phoned in to say they liked them. A few more people told me the same thing the next day. I've stuck with them ever since. It's my look, but not everybody likes it.

The day before the election, *Washington Post* TV critic Tom Shales scolded me in his column for not dressing better for interviews with the presidential and vice presidential candidates. Shales was especially offended that I hadn't put on a suit or a jacket to interview President Bush and his wife at the White House the previous month. "King is no slave to propriety, obviously," Shales wrote, "or to good taste."[1]

Fashion tips from ever-stylish print journalists are, of course, always appreciated. But I take critiques from the second-in-command of the free world even more seriously. During a May 1991 interview Vice President Quayle knocked my "pleasantly obnoxious" purple tie.

"You love this tie," I kidded him back. "You wish you wore this tie."

"Why don't you get conservative?" the telegenic Republican advised. "A nice, conservative gentleman's tie. And put a suit on next time."[2]

As much as he hated my tie, Quayle told our audience he would wear it to an Oval Office meeting the next day, which he did. He even sent me a picture of himself standing with Bush behind the president's desk. Bush is holding up my neckwear for the camera. He looks revolted. "What about this 'throw-up' tie?" Bush wrote on my copy of the photo. In return I let Quayle keep the tie—a gesture I'm still not sure he appreciates. "It's so ugly my kids like it," the former vice president says.[3]

At least Tucker and Benjamin Quayle have taste. Maybe I should send them suspenders for Christmas.

"Larry King Live" was criticized for many things during the 1992 campaign. And while I do not think my attire is a serious threat to the future of this democracy, I do have some concerns about the influence of talk shows on the political process.

The truth of the matter is that I am not a journalist. I have

never claimed to be. I'm an interviewer, a TV and radio personality—an entertainer. I'm no Ted Koppel. I want my audience to
learn something when they watch "Larry King Live" or listen to
me on the radio. But our viewers and listeners require that we
keep things moving, that we cover a lot of bases—that we keep
them entertained.

You can learn a lot about candidates by watching how they
react to the hustle and bustle of the talk shows. How does he think
on his feet? Is she answering the questions or spitting out prepro-
grammed answers that don't really mean anything? Is this someone
I trust, someone I like, someone I'd enjoy talking to? What does
he or she really care about? These are "character" questions. And
we can help answer them.

From a politician's point of view, a talk show is the electronic
version of what John Sununu calls "see-me-feel-me-touch-me"
campaigning. "I really believe the best way for a political candidate
to be able to communicate is to go directly" to the public, says the
former New Hampshire governor. "Get out there and go into the
malls. Let people look the candidate in the eye while he's . . .
talking about issues." In 1992 talk shows turned the whole country
into a small state where candidates could campaign living room to
living room, person to person, car radio to car radio. Talk shows,
Sununu says, are an "electronic mechanism" for old-fashioned "retail politics."[4]

Our show is more like a town meeting than a news conference.
I do not go into an interview as a reporter would, armed with
statistics to refute the latest political spin coming out of the White
House or Congress. I'm better at drawing people out than explaining policy. I know what I do best—and I've made a pretty good

living at it. But because I am not a journalist, I do not always ask the follow-up questions a reporter would ask. Often I leave it to others—the audience, the press—to decide if a candidate is deceiving them.

Bush, for instance, appeared on the show the Friday before the election, the same day the special prosecutor investigating the Iran-Contra scandal issued an indictment against former Defense Secretary Caspar Weinberger that raised questions about Bush's involvement in the arms-for-hostages scheme. Bush told me at the beginning of the program that the indictment was politically motivated. There was no "smoking gun" implicating him in the scandal, he said.[5]

George Stephanopoulos, the Clinton campaign's communications director, thought I had not pressed Bush hard enough on the Weinberger indictment, and he called Tammy in the control booth— via CNN in Atlanta—to complain. Tammy told Stephanopoulos that if he thought the president had not addressed the matter fully, he should say so on the air. Stephanopoulos resisted at first, but Tammy talked him into it and put him through to talk to Bush near the end of the show. Neither Bush nor I had any warning about the Stephanopoulos call. Tammy told me through my earpiece who the caller was as we were putting him on the air.

Stephanopoulos read from a Weinberger memo released with that day's indictment to refute Bush's contention that he had not known antitank missiles were being shipped to Iran in a direct effort to secure the release of U.S. hostages in Lebanon. "There was clearly an explicit deal of arms for hostages . . . ," Stephanopoulos said. "How could you not know that it was arms for hostages?"

Bush handled the unexpected on-air attack well. He recounted the young Clinton aide's résumé for the audience and complimented his work as spin master for the Clinton campaign. But he criticized him for engaging in "desperation, last-minute politics," I asked Stephanopoulos if he wanted to respond, but Bush cut him off.

"I didn't come here to debate Stephanopoulos," the president said. "I'm ready to debate you, Larry. Come on."

Bush's aides and advisers say he was furious about the Stephanopoulos call after the show that night. On the air he muttered sarcastically about Stephanopoulos getting through with a "random call," like viewers in Belgium and Switzerland who had questioned him earlier in the evening.

"We don't have a private number," I told Bush. "We really don't. I don't control the calls."[6]

Marlin Fitzwater says the president thought it was a setup. "It was a sandbag situation," the former White House spokesman says. "The president's sense of dignity and honor [was] offended by that."[7]

Of course, Bush and his aides had not complained when Rich Bond had done the same thing to Ross Perot in June. The Republican party chairman had phoned in during an interview with the independent candidate to challenge his claims about GOP dirty tricks. Such calls seemed fair to me at the time. Bond told his side, Perot told his; Stephanopoulos told his side, Bush told his. Dialogue is healthy and informative. But we will have to avoid turning our show into a staging ground for sneak attacks.

Rivals don't always phone in when they think one of my guests is pulling a fast one. In June, for instance, Bill Clinton told our viewers that he would "present a five-year plan to balance the budget" to Congress.[8] But none of the economic programs Clinton presented during the campaign—or since—included such a plan. And his campaign proposals for halving the deficit during his first term were never very specific. Maybe I should have pointed that out at the time.

I felt the same way after Vice President Quayle talked about the president's decision to break his "no new taxes" campaign pledge, during an interview in July 1992. Quayle offered one of the administration's most dubious explanations, linking the unpopular tax increases in the 1990 budget deal to that summer's crisis in the Persian Gulf. Bush went along with the "Democratic" tax increase, Quayle said, to prevent a "budget crisis" from interfering with the mobilization of U.S. troops in the Middle East.[9] But the Bush administration had agreed to raise taxes to cut the deficit that June, five weeks *before* Iraqi troops crossed the Kuwait border. Maybe I should have pointed that out, too.

But a show like "Larry King Live" may not be the best place for pressing candidates on budget plans or for the nuances of their health care plans—or for discussing the cost advantages of different types of solar panels for the space station, for that matter. That's a job for journalists. They should be the "referees" in the political process. Journalists have access to vast amounts of information most of the public would never have the time or inclination to weed through. So they can tell us when a candidate is fudging the truth, exaggerating, or lying.

That is why I am concerned when politicians try to use talk shows to circumvent the traditional press. And I worry even more when the public lets them get away with it. "You know why I can stiff you on the press conferences?" President Clinton asked an audience full of journalists in a speech at the Radio and Television Correspondents' Association Dinner in March 1993. "Because Larry King liberated me from you by giving me to the American people directly." He pointed to me in the audience. "There he is," Clinton said, "the person you ought to be mad at."[10] Of course, the president was half joking. But his audience was only half laughing.

Presidential candidates have always tried to avoid tough questions from reporters, especially during the general election campaign in the fall. For example, the last candidate for president to appear on NBC's "Meet the Press" after he won his party's nomination was George McGovern, the Democratic nominee in 1972. So the candidates' use of the talk shows, at least in the fall of 1992, was not "to our detriment," says NBC's Russert, "because they were never on our shows anyhow." But that is not a good thing. "If a candidate were to try to circumvent the mainstream press . . . and simply do the talk show circuit, I don't think that the candidate would be tested in a way that was necessary for the political process," the "Meet the Press" host says. "I personally believe that if you can't answer the tough questions, you will not be prepared to make the tough decisions."[11]

Talk shows and call-in programs are friendlier settings for a politician than Sunday morning shows with panels of hungry reporters. So talk shows let candidates use the media they like to avoid the media they do not like. By coming on "Larry King Live" or "Donahue," candidates can claim to be accessible. But voters need both kinds of media to make informed decisions. By not meeting the press, Clinton and the other candidates short-changed the public. Or, as Phil Donahue puts it, "If you're going to send my son or daughter to war and be brave enough to do that, you ought to be brave enough to face Bob Schieffer on 'Face the Nation.' "[12]

Donahue asked Clinton why he was avoiding the "mainstream" press during an interview in early October—the day after my bus-trip interview with Clinton and Al Gore in Ocala, Florida. "If you will forgive me," Clinton said, "I think going on a bus trip to Florida is more mainstream than going on 'Meet the Press' and 'Face the Nation.' And last night, we went on 'Larry King Live' and answered phoned-in questions. . . . I've been answering questions directly from the people. . . . I just don't let you guys filter me to the voters any more." Donahue's audience applauded Clinton's answer.[13]

Bush used a similar argument on "CBS This Morning" in July, when he answered questions from a live audience in the Rose Garden at the White House. The audience, picked from the White House tour line, asked Bush about the economy, health care, crime, trade, race relations, and so on. They were deferential—and nervous. Cohosts Harry Smith and Paula Zahn, on the other hand, pressed Bush on his broken promise in 1988 not to raise taxes, his administration's support for Saddam Hussein before he invaded Kuwait, Quayle's controversial Competitiveness Council, Ross Perot, and the president's standing in the polls.

"Why are these people not asking me all this?" Bush asked Zahn, gesturing to the audience. "It's you and Harry [who] have the controversial [questions]. . . . It's the correspondents [who ask] about Iraq or the polls or what I want to say about Ross Perot, when the American people want to know what I'm doing about . . . their problems."[14]

Bush cleverly dodged his hosts' questions by linking issues most of the public does not care about—such as his current standing in the polls—with issues the public should care about—such as his policy toward Iraq before the Gulf War. A squeeze play. I wonder if Bush's love of baseball helped him come up with such an artful dodge.

I follow politics the way I've followed baseball most of my life, which is not such an unusual combination, it turns out. Bush was captain of the baseball team at Yale, and his son is part owner of the Texas Rangers. George Will and David Broder—the two most-read political columnists in the country—are both fanatical baseball junkies as well. For those of us who follow both, baseball is often more rewarding than politics. There's a World Series every year, and the off-season is much shorter. But some fans care more about trivia—the stats, the records—than who won the game. Political reporters often focus on trivia, too—polls, strategy, and other insider stuff that does not interest most voters. And that allows candidates to make the questions and the questioners the issue, avoiding serious probing on serious issues.

Journalists and the public watch the candidates on talk shows for different reasons. The public may want to see what a candidate is like and hear what he has to say. Reporters, who hear what a candidate has to say over and over during a campaign, are waiting for "news" to happen. So when Bush came on our show for the second time in early October, it was "newsworthy" that he attacked Clinton with questions about the draft, his Moscow trip, and his participation in protests against the Vietnam War. Bush also talked about trade, the withdrawal of U.S. forces from Europe, health coverage for part-time federal employees—substantive things. But those weren't as newsworthy. Why? Because reporters need a "lead" for their story. A reporter cannot write, "Last night, the president appeared on 'Larry King Live' and talked about a great many things." That may be an accurate story, but who would want to read it. Sensational things, wacky things, gaffes, or attacks make better headlines—and better reading.

I rarely know what moment with a given guest will capture the attention of the press. Take, for instance, Quayle's appearance in July 1992—the night the vice president told me he would support his daughter if she decided to have an abortion (see pages 40–41). During that interview Quayle and I also talked about divided government. Democrats had controlled both chambers of Congress while a Republican occupied the White House for twenty of the past twenty-four years. If the public wanted to end gridlock in Washington, Quayle said, they should reelect the Republican administration and elect Republican majorities in both chambers of Congress.

But was the opposite also true?

"If you're going to vote for Bill Clinton," Quayle said, "I'd say vote for your Democratic congressman."

What a remarkable thing to say, I thought, especially since no one thought the Republicans would gain control of Congress. "In other words, the country would be better off if Bill Clinton is elected with a Democratic House and Senate," I said, "and if Bush is elected with a Republican House and Senate?"

"That is my viewpoint," Quayle responded.

"It may not be all your fellow Republicans' viewpoint."

"It's a controversial viewpoint . . . ," Quayle said, "and it's not shared by all the people in my party, but I think we must . . . have a united government." [15]

As we went off the air, I thought this exchange would be the big news story from our show that night. It was certainly the remark that most upset Bush's campaign managers, who thought the vice president had essentially told our viewers to vote for Clinton, Quayle recalls.[16] Instead the press focused on Quayle's remarks about abortion and his daughter. Abortion is a more sensational issue than divided government.

I don't mind making news, of course, but the things that make news often seem pretty inane. Bush shows me his driver's license on the air. Tipper Gore phones in anonymously to ask her husband out on a date. Did these moments make news because they were entertaining, or are we looking for entertaining moments to make news—or both? Why do news organizations cover these things? For the same reason we put them on the air. Talk-show hosts and journalists are simultaneously in the information business and the entertainment business. We are "infotainers." But how low will we go?

I do not expect to see a presidential candidate on "Geraldo" any time soon, but I wouldn't be surprised if a syndicated TV tabloid like "Hard Copy" or "Inside Edition"—or one of the highly rated prime-time network copies, such as NBC's "Dateline"—breaks a major political scandal in the near future. After all, the big scandal of the 1992 campaign, Clinton's alleged affair with Gennifer Flowers, started in a supermarket tabloid.

Donahue and I certainly gave Geraldo Rivera a run for his money once or twice during the '92 campaign. I helped spread completely unsubstantiated rumors about Clinton when I asked the Arkansas governor in October if he had ever considered renouncing his citizenship. "Never," Clinton said.

"Where did that [rumor] start from?" I asked.

Clinton laughed. "You tell me." [17]

Those rumors were started by Republicans, but I had just spread them.

In an April interview Donahue quizzed Democratic primary candidate Jerry Brown on his marital status—and, through innuendo, his sexual orientation. "If you want to know, do I go out with girls? Yes, I do," Brown said. "You want their names and their phone numbers? They're probably watching this show." [18]

It was Brown's second appearance on "Donahue" in as many weeks, and the second time the host had challenged him on this subject. The previous week, Donahue had suggested that Brown's single, "monk-like persona" was contributing to his image as a "flake." If he "had somebody standing there smiling up at [him], your lady . . . like all candidates are supposed to do," he'd be taken more seriously. "Where is the joy of life . . . ?" Donahue asked. "Where's the fun? Where's the self-deprecating humor?"

"Well," Brown said, "I wouldn't have gotten on this show if I didn't have a good sense of humor." [19]

That's entertainment! That does not, however, serve democracy. When talk shows delve into rumor and innuendo, we hurt the political process—just as the traditional press does when it pursues such matters. Maybe we can't help it.

"Television is basically an entertainment medium," says Michael Deaver, Ronald Reagan's longtime image czar. "Everybody keeps forgetting that. We have to be constantly aroused or excited or entertained by television, and that includes television news. . . . Because we get all this information [visually] . . . it has to be something that grabs us every day or we . . . watch soaps or something else."

Does that mean politicians must now be entertainers? Deaver says no. But "the candidate has to be presented in an attractive, entertaining way," he says, "or he's not going to get anyplace." [20]

Politicians did their best to be entertaining in 1992. The week of the Democratic National Convention, Bill and Hillary Clinton posed with their daughter Chelsea for the cover of *People* magazine, a publication that usually keeps us up to date on the trials and tribulations of the stars. This is where we turn to read about Burt Reynolds's and Loni Anderson's divorce, or the latest on Princess Di, or to find out about "the sexiest man alive." *People* tells us what the stars' lives are *really* like. And the Clinton campaign had very specific reasons for wanting their candidate and his family to appear on its cover and in its pages that week.

"That was at a point where people really didn't know he had a daughter," media adviser Mandy Grunwald says. "And that was because the Clintons are so protective of Chelsea. They didn't want to use her as a prop for the campaign or things that other political families do to their children. But as a result people did not see this side of his life which is so important to him." [21]

So, did they use Chelsea as a prop? *People*'s private scenes in the governor's mansion in Little Rock were extremely helpful to Clinton, whose family life had been an issue during the primaries. But exposing *People*'s readers to the private Bill Clinton—the side of him they may not have heard about during the Gennifer Flowers flap—also contributed to the trend that helped generate the Flowers controversy in the first place.

Politicians are becoming more like celebrities, appearing in *People* or on our show to plug their candidacies as if they were promoting a new film, book, or record. So it was not strange for me to sit with President Bush and say to the viewers, "See you tomorrow night with Suzanne Somers and Whoopi Goldberg," or, "Monday night Robert Redford will be [our] guest," or to have Cher call Ross Perot on the show and volunteer for his campaign.[22] They're all in the same business now.

Politicians already campaign—and raise funds—with celebrities. The Clinton campaign headlined with Barbra Streisand. Bush rolled out his own big guns, turning Bruce Willis and Arnold Schwarzenegger loose on the campaign trail. And one of these days I'm sure a political figure will call in to our show to talk to a star— and maybe even ask for an endorsement.

Having star power can help a campaign. But by acting like celebrities, candidates expose themselves to celebrity questions. The public begins to wonder about politicians' personal lives, as they wonder about other stars, which produces stories like the Gennifer Flowers scandal. Is any of this good for the political process? Does having star power make it any easier to balance the budget, to design and pass a health care plan, or to serve as commander in chief and leader of the free world? Or does it make it harder?

Regardless, in politics the stars don't always sparkle. The public enjoyed watching candidate Clinton play his saxophone on the "Arsenio Hall Show," but they were unsympathetic when President Clinton caught flak from the press for inviting so many celebrities to the White House and for getting a two hundred dollar haircut on Air Force One from Christophe, one of Hollywood's top stylists. The voters have their limits.

Another major concern is crazy callers. We have never screened calls on my radio show, so I usually don't know who the caller is or what the question will be. They are just the city ("Syracuse, you're on . . ."). I wish it was that way on CNN, but TV time is too precious. Two producers sit in a small booth off the control room at our studio in Washington answering calls on eight lines. They decide with the producer in charge which callers to go with.

Like politicians, we have to tolerate a certain amount of idiosyncrasy from our callers. Nixon has said that politics requires tolerance for "oddballs and bores." To prove his point he describes New York govenor Thomas Dewey dismissing a drunken, back-slapping guest at a 1952 Republican fund-raising dinner with a deliberate flick of his cigarette. "Who was that fatuous ass?" Dewey asked. As it turned out, the man was the publisher of a string of weekly newspapers.

"Like many brilliant people, Dewey found it very difficult to tolerate fools," Nixon wrote in his 1990 memoir, *In the Arena.* "In politics, that is a fatal mistake for three reasons. First, the man might not be a fool. Second, even fools vote. And third, a fool might still have something worthwhile to say to you."[23]

We have better luck than a lot of shows in weeding out the silly, pointless, rambling, and embarrassing calls, in part because our producers deal with hundreds of callers night after night. We can usually—but certainly not always—spot the strange ones, even the followers of radio "shock jock" Howard Stern. Stern's fans often.pose as serious callers with serious questions in order to say their master's name on TV. Stern then replays such moments on his radio show. The lengths these callers will go to and the ruses they will come up with to get on the air always surprises me. We missed one Stern prankster, for instance, during a September 1992 interview with Marilyn Quayle. Disaster relief was one of the Second Lady's pet issues, and Mrs. Quayle was joining us from south Florida, where she was on a fact-finding trip to assess federal relief work following Hurricane Andrew. Our second caller that night was from Egg Harbor, New Jersey. "Mrs. Quayle," he said, "I was a victim of the 1972 Hurricane Agnes in Wilkes-Barre, Pennsylvania. I lost everything . . . I had. I'd like to know what you think of Howard Stern." [24]

Stern's fans often know what sort of questions interest the producers who decide which callers get to ask questions. One slipped past the "screeners" at NBC's "Today" show during a June call-in with Clinton. "What do you think of Howard Stern?" the caller from Albany, New York, asked.

Clinton laughed. "I don't know how to answer that."

The question the caller used to beat the gatekeepers in the control room at NBC: "What do you think of the talk-show circuit's effect on the political process?" [25]

Two days later, when Ross Perot was in Clinton's seat on "Today," the first questioner turned out to be another Stern follower. "I have a two-part question," the caller said. "First of all, is it realistic that an outsider can go to Washington and convince Congress to make major changes in the government? And secondly, have you ever had the desire to mind-meld with Howard Stern's penis?"

Perot looked befuddled, but host Katie Couric was quick as ever. "Oh, thank you very much," she said. "Not a good second question, but let's go ahead and ask the first." [26]

One of the only guests I've ever had who has taken a Stern caller seriously was the ever-earnest Al Gore. During my July 1992 interview with the senator at the Democratic convention, Gore was actually apologetic when a caller from Huntington, New York, wanted to know how he felt about Stern and he did not have an answer. "You may not believe this," the senator said, "but I don't think I've ever really listened to him."

I laughed, "You join a list of many,"[27]

The ultra-conservative stars of talk radio generally do not offend me as much as Stern, whose jokes all seem to be about lesbians or various bodily excretions. But I am not much of a fan of conservative Rush Limbaugh's program, either. Limbaugh has built huge audiences for himself by railing against "femi-nazis" and other liberals. There is a big audience for right-leaning talk radio, as a 1993 survey by the Times Mirror Center for the People & the Press found. About 25 percent of those polled who called themselves conservatives said they regularly listened to talk radio, compared with 11 percent of the liberals.[28] The talk radio audience is especially conservative during the day. I've really noticed the difference since my radio show moved from nights to days in 1993. It's a demographic phenomenon. Many of those who are home in the afternoon listening to the show—housewives and seniors, for example—tend to be more conservative about a lot of issues. But even the most right-leaning members of my new daytime audience are moderates compared with the people I sometimes hear on Limbaugh's show.

Talk shows like Limbaugh's appeal to the worst in us—the selfishness, the anger, the fear. It's soap box pap, a primal response to this country's many social problems—satisfying for a moment perhaps, but ultimately unproductive. It's too reactionary for me. I do not respond well to extremists. It has nothing to do with Limbaugh's political views. It's just the way he presents them. I'd say the same thing if he was a liberal. Paul Harvey is conservative and I love listening to him. The writing is brilliant and his delivery is perfect.

I am a Brooklyn Democrat brought up on Franklin Roosevelt

and Harry Truman. That's certainly no secret to anyone who has ever heard my radio show, especially when I open the phones to chat with listeners about whatever they want to talk about. It's hard not to have an opinion on a radio talk show. If somebody asks me if I'm pro-choice, for instance, I have to tell them I am. If they ask what I think about some political figure, I feel like I have to answer. But if we did not do open phones like that, you'd never hear my opinions. I try to keep them out of my interviews as much as I can.

Limbaugh once asked me why I am called a "broadcast personality" and he is called a "right-wing" talk-show host. Was this just another example of liberal media bias? Actually, the answer has more to do with style than slant. I'm more interested in my guest's opinions than mine. I'm as nice to Dan Quayle as I am to Al Gore. Critics might say I'm too soft on both of them. So be it. I like putting people at ease. I'm not out to embarrass my guests. As an interviewer, I am neither left nor right, conservative or liberal. I am just curious. When I'm thinking of questions, I try to put myself in my guest's shoes. I want to know what and how they think. I do not want to provoke them.

I do not think Limbaugh is a dangerous person. But I do get nervous sometimes listening to his show, and shows like it. When I hear an extremist—liberal or conservative—barking on radio or television I often wonder if there is an audience out there for a political candidate like that, a new-age Joe McCarthy. The late Wisconsin senator was able to get away with so much for so long and ruin so many lives before Murrow and the Army-McCarthy hearings finally put an end to his demagogic campaign against communism. I worry about a slicker, TV-savvy McCarthy coming along someday. A charming demagogue who is good on camera and good at saying what people like to hear could use talk shows to tap public support and rise to power. People in politics tell me not to worry. They tell me to trust the viewers to see through such a person. The camera catches up with everybody, they say.

Michael Deaver recalls asking Reagan once about Dick Powell, the actor. "Tell me about him," Deaver said. "Was he as great a guy as I think he was?"

"Mike, you're always asking me about these actors," Reagan answered. "Let me tell you something, the camera doesn't lie. Dick Powell was a great guy and you know it. There are other guys [who] are jerks, and you know that, too. You can't fool the camera."

Deaver thinks Reagan's rule is as true in politics as it is in the movies or on television—especially with camera crews trailing candidates and presidents around the clock. "The camera doesn't lie," Deaver says. "We see too much of you."[29]

Gary Hart, whose second campaign for president in 1988 ended after newspaper reports about his personal life, agrees. "The best way to weed out the phonies is not to trust the *Washington Post* or the *Miami Herald* to do it, but trust the American people to do it . . . ," he says. "Let them talk to the candidate. Let them ask the questions they want to ask, not the questions the editors and the journalists want to ask. . . . And believe me, you put a phony or a shallow, hollow, unqualified person on enough television, they'll sink themselves."[30]

I did not see anything during the presidential campaign that proved Hart or Deaver wrong. David Duke, the Louisiana state representative and former Ku Klux Klan leader, was not any more popular with Republican primary voters in 1992 than he was with our audience when he came on the show during his losing guber-natorial campaign in 1991. That's comforting. And yet I still worry that we are vulnerable to manipulation, that a truly dangerous politician could come along and the public would like what they saw.

Vice President Gore, a former reporter, says television viewers are increasingly aware of political "artifice and manipulation." But, he adds, "New and ever-more elaborate approaches to try to present candidates as something they are not will, of course, continue to pose risks, but that's part of the democratic process and always will be."[31]

Don Wright, The Palm Beach Post.

Air Power

BY THE FIRST MONDAY in November I was ready for a break from politics. And after back-to-back interviews the previous week with the three major presidential contenders and Vice President Quayle, I thought the audience could use a break, too. So I was greatly relieved when our producers booked Robert Redford as the show's election-eve guest.

But Redford is active in the conservation movement. Preserving our nation's rivers and resources was a theme in the film he was plugging—*A River Runs Through It,* his latest directorial outing. So I couldn't help but ask the star what he thought about President Bush, the self-proclaimed "environmental president," mocking Al Gore's earthy ideas. "Ozone man," Bush had called the senator.

Redford was angry about it. He admonished Bush for trying to "score some shallow point, when in truth [environmental issues are] too serious to make a joke about. . . . The fact that he can't take it seriously enough . . . I think is pathetic."

That said, I wanted to move on. This was supposed to be a respite from politics. But our audience had their own political questions for the actor. The first caller, a woman from Maryland, wanted to know if Redford would ever consider running for office.

Redford borrowed Perot's old "temperament" answer. "It would not suit me . . . ," he said. "I don't think that I would be a good politician because I don't find compromise that easy, and I would have a lot more fun doing what I'm doing."

A caller from Zurich, Switzerland, wanted to know how Redford felt when people said Dan Quayle looked like him. Some Bush advisers in 1988 had thought Quayle's Redford-like looks would make him a young and attractive addition to the GOP ticket. But instead of the wholesome hero type, Quayle critics were reminded of the naive senatorial challenger Redford portrayed in *The Candidate*. What did the actor think?

"Well," he said, "it was insulting."

"You were insulted by the comparison?"

"I can't think of any other way to put it," Redford said. "Let me try another way, it was *really* insulting."

The Democrats couldn't have asked for a nicer endorsement.

"Everyone else is doing it," I said, "so we might as well get yours. Predictions for tomorrow?"

"I wouldn't predict," Redford said. "I can only give you my hope."

"Which is?"

"Well, I don't want to wake up . . . and look to another four years of the same thing, where we have such a drastic cost of human consequences. I certainly don't want that."

There was no escaping the campaign. It was all anyone wanted to talk about—and not just in this country. Redford was stunned that someone from Switzerland would call to ask him about Quayle.

"We're all over the world, Bob . . . ," I told him. "We're in a hundred and fifty-one countries."

"That's great . . . ," Redford said. "And by the way, I'll tell you why I think that's great. Not to turn this into a 'your turn to curtsy, my turn to bow' here, but I really do like the idea that there is a show where the public can have direct access to . . . political leaders. I think that's great."[1]

That, of course, is what talk-show democracy is all about: access producing interest. Talk shows made politics accessible to millions of voters and nonvoters who felt disenfranchised. In the final weeks of the campaign, you could hardly turn on your television without finding one of the candidates answering people's questions on one program or another. It was "dial-a-candidate" politics.

The Friday before the election "Good Morning America" took over the Candlewick Diner in East Rutherford, New Jersey, for an hour-long town meeting with Bill Clinton. Clinton took questions from fourteen breakfasting patrons ABC lined up as cohost Charlie Gibson jumped from table to table with his microphone:

"Let's go on over to the next table. . . .

"We've got some more tables to cover here on this side of the diner. . . .

"Let's turn to a gentleman who seems to be having a salami-and-cheese breakfast here. . . ."[2]

It takes a strange presidential race to turn a well-paid TV personality into a waiter.

The 1992 campaign was the first time I can remember there being more interest in an election at the end of the process than at the beginning. At the start of the campaign Bush seemed unbeatable. In the final weeks he seemed unelectable. Ross Perot had reentered the race, capturing many of the moderate voters who might have helped the president come from behind. Perot stripped some support from Clinton, too, and the polls were narrowing. But the Arkansas governor fought hard to maintain his lead. He was "robo-candidate," campaigning virtually nonstop from town to town, talk show to talk show.

Huge audiences—more than eighty million viewers—tuned in for each of the presidential and vice presidential debates. Millions of viewers also watched Perot's paid, half-hour "infomercials." And the ratings were unusually high whenever a candidate appeared on television for an interview or call-in session. At "Larry King Live" our ratings for candidate appearances rivaled our audiences during the Gulf War, when much of the world was glued to CNN. The campaign became a sort of miniseries—perhaps as big as "Roots" or "The Thorn Birds." Viewers tuned in nightly to find out what was going to happen to Bill, George, and Ross. We were all on a first-name basis by then. We knew them that well.

More than 104 million Americans voted in the 1992 presidential election, the largest turnout ever. That was up 14 percent from 91.6 million voters in 1988—the biggest increase in forty years. It was also the highest percentage turnout among eligible voters since the Kennedy-Nixon race in 1960. Exit polls showed that 11 percent of those voting were pulling the lever in an election for the first time. And if anyone doubts their impact, consider this: just under half of these first-time voters—about 5.5 million people—supported Clinton. That accounted for nearly all of Clinton's 5.8 million vote margin.[3]

In 1992 political alienation turned into frustration. And the high voter turnout was a by-product of the same anger that made talk shows so important that year. The public was angry about gridlock in Washington, about a government that seemed unable or unwilling to address mounting problems. They were nervous about the economy. The recession may not have been as deep or difficult as many others since World War II, as the Bush campaign tried vainly to remind voters. But economic uncertainty was more intense than ever. People were tired of election-year promises candidates never intended to keep. And they were fed up with politicians who thought meeting with contributors was more important than meeting with constituents.

In speeches during the Democratic primaries, Jerry Brown often asked his audience to raise their hands if they had ever given a political candidate at least one thousand dollars. Few people ever had. No one here has given that much money, Brown would say, but the people who have are the ones who really run the government. It was one of Brown's best bits. By tapping this anti-Washington sentiment—with populist rhetoric, his 800 number, and a self-imposed one hundred dollar limit on campaign contributions—Brown kept his candidacy alive longer than any of Clinton's other rivals in the primaries.

Much of the public felt the country was being run by a small group of people living comfortably under a bubble on the banks of the Potomac. And the press, for the most part, seemed locked under that dome, too. The voices outside were muffled, inaudible. Talk shows were like a glass cutter, a way for the public to reach the people under the bubble.

For most people, of course, this was a vicarious process. Millions of people watched the candidates on "Larry King Live" in 1992, but only about ten dozen actually reached the presidential and vice presidential contenders on our show. In a July 1993 poll by the Times Mirror Center, only 11 percent of those surveyed said they had ever called a talk show, and only 6 percent of the respondents said they had ever talked on the air.[4]

But people did not have to pick up the phone themselves to feel empowered. Just seeing the telephone number on their TV screens or hearing it on their radios, knowing they could call if they wanted to, hearing other people voice their own fears and frustrations was liberating enough.

The people who do call in to talk shows are more frustrated with government and the status qou than society on the whole, as the Times Mirror Center poll suggests. But they are still able spokesmen and spokeswomen for widespread public sentiment. And, for a candidate or office holder, understanding their feelings is good politics. Cuomo says, "If the voice you hear on the call-in show is more emphatically negative than the public at large, okay. But still you come away with a distinct feeling that there are a lot of people, even if they're not 51 percent, who are very unhappy. And that's significant, and the reason for their unhappiness is significant, whether you think they're right or wrong."[5]

Talk shows also showed the public that *they* were responsible for many of the nation's problems, as Perot repeatedly reminded audiences during his campaign. "Who's at fault?" he asked rhetorically during a March 1992 speech at Washington's National Press

Club. "First thing you've got to do in our country is blame somebody, right? Well, go home tonight and look in the mirror. . . .
You and I are at fault because we own this country, and there is
the problem in a nutshell. We've abdicated our ownership responsibilities."[6]

In many ways talk shows were the mirror Perot spoke of.
Gridlock begins at home, as our callers often proved. They would
phone in to complain about how wasteful and undisciplined the
government was. Cut spending! Balance the budget! But any ideas
for doing either provoked just as many complaints. Don't cut my
benefits! Don't close my local military base or slash funding for
my pet project! And don't you dare raise my taxes! Damned if you
do, and damned if you don't. No wonder Washington seemed to
be spinning its wheels.

Among Clinton's budget-cutting ideas, for instance, was a proposal to reduce administrative overhead for federally sponsored
university research. But even this modest idea provoked a typical
call from a concerned research administrator from Yale when Clinton was on our show in early October. "I wonder if you realize
what the implications are to the continuation of medical research
in the country if you're successful in saving almost a billion dollars
on university research," the caller said. "Also, the implications to
people's jobs—namely, mine."[7]

Clinton said that by cutting administrative costs, he hoped to
free more funds for actual research. I'm sure that was little con-
solation to the administrator, who was understandably preoccupied with his own livelihood. But voters generally began to recognize
that they would have to straighten themselves out and agree to
sacrifice if they really wanted the government to straighten itself
out. That message fueled the Perot movement, as it had Paul

Tsongas's candidacy in the Democratic primaries. It rang true even among those who would never vote for Perot. There were plenty of people who thought Perot did not have the answers. But no one asked the questions better than he did.

Perot told voters they had to take back the political process— from special interests, from the press. And call-in programs gave them a tool with which to do it. Talk shows meant anyone with a phone had the sort of direct access to candidates they thought only lobbyists could buy. They asked the questions. They set the agenda.

"Voters wanted to hear from the candidates themselves," Clinton strategist James Carville says. They wanted "to know what so and so is saying, not what somebody said they were saying. . . . Talk shows offered that."[8]

Talk shows also offered the candidates more than the nine seconds they typically got each night on the news to make their case. A candidate could ramble at length on any subject. And because their positions did not have to be explained in less than a third of the time of your average beer commercial, candidates could afford to take risks. They could take difficult stands, unpopular positions, knowing that they would have time to explain themselves. Clinton could talk about raising taxes. Perot could talk about cutting popular programs. And Bush could try to explain why the economy was not in as bad shape as much of the public thought it was.

Talk shows were also an alternative to the thirty-second attacks that dominate political advertising. The increasing nastiness of campaigns was a major factor in the public's rejection of the political system before 1992. Negative campaigning actually discourages participation by giving people reasons not to vote for a particular candidate. It is much easier to convince people not to vote for someone than it is to get them to switch their vote. So, in the cynical mathematics of political mud-wrestling, if I convince more of your voters to stay home than you do mine, I win.

These tactics fall flat on talk shows. Callers and viewers want to know why they should vote *for* you, not why they shouldn't vote for your opponent. When Quayle came on our show in July, a week after the Democratic National Convention, he was predictably critical of Clinton and Gore and promised to focus on their "vulnerabilities." He talked about "family values." He talked about Clinton's plans to raise taxes. "I'm . . . going to tell the truth about Bill Clinton and Al Gore," he promised. "They don't like being called liberal, but they are liberal."

Our first caller that night was not impressed. "I see that you all are focusing on Mr. Clinton's and Mr. Gore's campaign . . . ," he said to the vice president. "When are you going to get off their campaign and talk about what [you are] going to do to make the country better?"

Quayle answered by briefly summing up Bush's economic proposals, but then turned back to the Democratic ticket. "You've got to remind people . . . what Bill Clinton and Al Gore are all about," Quayle said. "They come out of New York City and they say, 'We are these raging moderates.' That is a bunch of hooey. You know, Al Gore's voting record is the same as Ted Kennedy. Now, is Ted Kennedy a moderate? No. Bill Clinton as governor of Arkansas . . . [raised] taxes something like 128 different times. His record down there is not a record of moderation. . . . This is a trick. I mean, it was a slick convention, and I congratulate them for it. . . . But they are trying to paint themselves as moderates, and they are not moderates. They may be able to fool the people of New York City, but they cannot be allowed to fool the American people."[9]

In one tirade Quayle craftily conjured up several of the Republicans' favorite bogeymen: liberals, Ted Kennedy, taxes, even New York City. But in doing so he seemed to prove the caller's point. Quayle was better at explaining what was wrong with the Democratic nominees than what was good about the Republican administration. Our audience seemed to want something more.

But talk shows did not just serve the public. Carville says the "alternative" media were good hunting grounds for candidates seeking support. The audiences who tuned in to the traditional outlets for political news, such as the networks' Sunday morning interview shows, were mostly "people who are pretty interested in public affairs and [who] don't tend to be very undecided," he says.[10] In other words, Clinton would have a better chance of reaching the people he needed to reach—people who might vote for him, not people who already knew they would or who knew they wouldn't—on "Larry King Live" or the "Arsenio Hall Show" than on "Meet the Press."

Candidates do have to be careful and selective in their use of alternative media. A member of the cast of "Saturday Night Live" once asked Paul Tsongas if he would consider hosting the show. After a few days Tsongas decided this informal invitation was not in his best interests as a candidate. "I was trying to present myself as a serious truth teller," he says. But it was a tough decision. "It's funny," he says. "I'm in the middle of a campaign, and all I'm thinking about is my opening monologue. . . . And it was difficult to say no because I'd already developed the monologue, and I thought it was pretty funny."[11]

Mandy Grunwald, the media consultant who proposed that Clinton appear on "Arsenio Hall," says she would not be surprised if a candidate "self-destructs" in 1996 trying to repeat the Arkansas governor's late-night coup. "Often what happens is people repeat the tactical success of past campaigns instead of understanding the strategic imperative for them . . . ," she explains. "We needed to explain to people who Bill Clinton was, what his life was about, what he was about, what he was about in personal terms. We had a strategic mandate to do that."[12] And Clinton was charming enough to pull it off. Another candidate in another circumstance might look foolish.

Generally speaking, though, the rise of talk shows and other unconventional media outlets for political information is good for the process, and even good for the traditional press, because it creates more interest in the candidates and the issues. Viewers who see Clinton on "Arsenio Hall" are unlikely to cast their vote simply because they think he plays a mean sax. But by playing the saxophone he may interest those viewers enough to want to find out more about his candidacy. The same was true for call-in shows.

"My selfish view on all this is that the more people get exposed to politics and hooked on it, then the more likely they'll be to gravitate towards 'Meet the Press' . . . and the more traditional programs," Russert says, adding that his show's ratings went up "considerably" during the 1992 campaign. "We were the beneficiary, I believe, of a lot of people who were pulled into the process who normally wouldn't have been exposed to it. But they watch 'Larry King' on a nightly basis, they watch all the Hollywood stars and all the other people that [go on] that program, and they get hooked on the politics, too. Maybe it was just a spectator sport . . . but it is not something that is going to be hurtful."[13]

Candidates' extended exposure to the audience on call-in shows also helped voters make judgments about them as people. The conversational setting is different from the confrontational approach of some journalistic programs. On talk shows politicians can relax and act like living, breathing human beings, instead of scarred and callous pols going into battle. Both approaches have their merits. And, as a candidate appears repeatedly in both formats, his or her constituents can develop a rounded impression. "The longer [a] person is in your living room," Gary Hart says, "the more you can decide for yourself whether he or she makes any sense, is telling the truth, is of sound character, and all the qualities you want for national leadership."[14]

Such an opportunity might have helped Hart in May 1987, when he withdrew from the Democratic presidential primaries amid press questions about his private life. The *Miami Herald* had reported that the former Colorado senator spent a weekend with model Donna Rice in his Washington town house, and other news organizations were also pursuing rumors about his extramarital activities. Some in Hart's campaign proposed buying a block of television time for Hart to tell his side of the story, but he decided against it and ended his candidacy.

Could Hart have remained a candidate and used talk shows to bypass scandal-hungry reporters? He doesn't think so. "There was too much chaos then . . . ," he says. "It was made clear to me that it was not going to end. It wasn't one incident that made my decision. It was the clear signal from portions of the media that they were just not going to let up. . . . If I'd been Perot I could have bought all the [air] time in the world and they still wouldn't have left me alone. . . . There was no way out of it."[15]

I'm not so sure. The public is more forgiving than many politicians think. Admission—even partial admission—works, as Clinton showed when he was asked "Gary Hart" questions in 1992, or as Richard Nixon showed me during a January 1992 interview.

"Is it hard to come back to this city?" I asked the former president. "Is it hard to drive by the Watergate?"

"Well, I've never been in the Watergate," Nixon said.

"Never been in?"

"No," he said. "Other people were in there, though—unfortunately."[16] That regret, that self-deprecating humor, was very disarming.

The conversational tone of a talk show and its humanizing effect are perfectly suited for a politician who is in trouble. John Sununu had to resign as Bush's White House chief of staff in 1991 after he was repeatedly skewered in the press for abusing White House travel perks. The day Sununu resigned he was on the road with Bush. He called me from *Air Force One* to ask if he could come on the show that night and tell his side of the story. "I wanted to explain [the resignation] directly to people rather than let it get translated" through the press, he said.[17]

The chance to communicate directly, unfiltered by the press, is talk TV's biggest draw for politicians. Perot says that live, unedited programs "allow a person to say what he or she wants to say in their own words without having it rephrased. Then the viewer, I think, without any question feels that they're getting it straight . . . . My favorite expression [in edited interviews] has been that my answer would be printed correctly, but they would change the question." [18]

Some talk show critics miss the filter. They say callers often ask "softball" questions. But Perot knows better than most how tough audiences can be on a candidate. On NBC's "Today" show in June, he answered a call from "Roberta" in Vero Beach, Florida, who wanted to know if Perot planned to eliminate Social Security benefits for those earning more than sixty thousand dollars a year.

Perot said that wealthy Americans had to sacrifice to preserve the American dream. "Like when you and I were young, in the [Great] Depression, things were very bad," he said. "But we had a dream, and it's best expressed . . . in the song from *Annie.*" Perot then launched into a chorus of "Tomorrow." "Isn't it sad now [that] your grandchildren, my grandchildren, are wondering if they will have the American dream, too?"

"Today" cohost Katie Couric asked Roberta if she was satisfied with Perot's answer.

"Well," Roberta said, "he didn't really answer the question."

"Well, what do you want me to answer?" Perot asked, a little flustered.

"I wondered if you really are going to not give people [earning more than sixty thousand dollars a year] any Social Security benefits?"

Perot said he had never suggested such a thing, but that he would ask people like himself, "who just don't need" their Social Security benefits, to give them up "voluntarily." "I think there are many, many people who will say, 'If that will help, I'll give it up.' "

"Well, you can afford to give it up," Roberta said.

"That's the criteria, people who can afford to give it up."

"Who are those people, Mr. Perot?" Roberta asked.

"Let's go make the computer runs and define it," he said. "This is a rational analysis."[19]

As Perot found out, people can be tough interrogators when they feel their livelihoods are on the line. It has much more impact when a senior calls to ask about her benefits, or when an unemployed person asks what you're going to do to get him a job, than it does when Sam Donaldson or I ask about Social Security or unemployment. "Those of us who regard ourselves as hard news reporters do not have a copyright on asking good questions," Bernard Shaw says. "Some of the best questions in campaign '92 came from voters."[20] That was never more true than when the presidential candidates borrowed the talk-show format for one of their debates in the fall.

The idea of using the talk-show format for a debate came up early in the campaign year, when "Donahue" hosted Brown and Clinton together on the eve of the April 7 primaries in New York and Wisconsin. But Donahue did not make his audience part of that encounter. In fact, he did not even participate himself. "I am pleased to present Governor Brown [and] Governor Clinton," he said simply at the beginning of the program, and then turned the rest of the hour over to his two guests. There was no studio audience that day and the host sat silently—on the set but just off camera.[21] Donahue says that he actually wanted to leave the set entirely, but the Clinton campaign would not let him.[22]

Brown and Clinton asked each other questions and were surprisingly genteel after the nasty charges and countercharges they had leveled at each other in the preceding days. No real blows were exchanged. No blood was spilled. In fact, they spent most of the hour discussing the issues they agreed on and criticizing the Republican administration. At the end of the program, Donahue thanked his guests as simply as he introduced them ("Gentlemen, thank you both."), and that was it.[23] This relatively tame event was well received. And, as Donahue put it in an op-ed piece in the *Washington Post* the following September, "Only the boldest employee in my office suggested [that] the rave reviews may have been prompted" by the host's low profile.

In his *Post* piece Donahue suggested a similar, "hermetically sealed . . . media-less" debate between Bush and Clinton. "No moderator, no audience, no press, no phone calls," Donahue suggested. "No Tom, Peter, Dan, Bernie. . . . No Diane, no Robin, no Sam, no Cokie. No Phil. Just the two of them, alone together."[24] That would have been interesting. Clinton, however, had his own idea for using the talk-show format to take on Bush.

On September 30, 1992, when CNN announced that the president would appear on "Larry King Live" the following Sunday, the Bush and Clinton campaigns were still haggling with each other over the debates—when, where, how many, what format? Perot would go along with whatever they decided. Clinton had already won this "debate" debate, portraying Bush as cowardly for rejecting a bipartisan commission's proposal for four face-offs with a single moderator at each. The Democrats even sent a guy in a chicken suit to trail the president from campaign event to campaign event.

Clinton used the "Larry King Live" announcement as another opportunity to challenge Bush to debate him—this time on our show! "Then we get the best of all worlds," Clinton said, "one

moderator and millions of questioners."[25] White House spokesman Marlin Fitzwater immediately rejected Clinton's challenge.
Clinton wants to debate, Fitzwater said, then he wants to go on
"Larry King Live." Next Clinton will "be wanting to go on 'Arsenio Hall' and the 'Gong Show' again."[26]

I never expected the Bush campaign to accept Clinton's invitation. By then, I was just glad the president had finally agreed to
appear on our show. Ironically, though, Bush and one of his most
senior campaign advisers have told me separately that the president's campaign suggested me as a potential debate panelist or
moderator in talks with Clinton's people. I was told that the Democrats vetoed the idea, but maybe Bush was just stroking me. Oh,
well. I'll admit, it would have been fun.

The Bush and Clinton campaigns finally agreed to hold four
debates, three presidential and one vice presidential. And at Clinton's urging the second debate was a talk-show-style town meeting.
More than two hundred undecided voters from the Richmond,
Virginia, area would quiz the three presidential contenders. Moderator Carole Simpson of ABC News had less than a week to pre-
pare for the difficult event. "I was really worried about it because
I hadn't really done anything like that," she says.[27]

The key moment of the Richmond debate was when a woman
in the audience asked the three candidates how the "national debt"
affected them personally. "And if it hasn't," she said, "how can
you honestly find a cure for the economic problems of the common people, if you have no experience in what's ailing them?"
While not worded exactly right, this was the central question of
the 1992 election: Tell me you know how much we're hurting.

Perot said his concern about the national debt was what had

inspired him to run for president in the first place. "It caused me to disrupt my private life and my business to get involved in this activity," he said. "That's how much I care about it. And believe me, if you knew my family and if you knew the private life I have, you would agree in a minute that that's a whole lot more fun than getting involved in politics." But the questioner did not mean the "national debt" literally. She was asking about the nation's economic problems in general.

Bush did not understand the question either. He started his answer by talking about how interest rates, which are affected by the debt, are important to everyone.

"You, on a personal basis," the woman interrupted. "How has it affected you?"

Bush still did not understand the question. He looked confused and uncomfortable, as he had throughout most of the night—fidgeting, looking at his watch. It was almost painful watching him struggle to understand what this woman wanted to know. "Are you suggesting that if somebody has means that the national debt doesn't affect them? . . ." he asked. "I'm not sure it get [it]—help me with the question, and I'll try to answer it."

There was a murmur of disbelief in the audience. He didn't *get* it?

"Well," the woman said, "I've had friends that have been laid off from jobs. . . . I know people who cannot afford to pay the mortgage on their homes, their car payment. I have personal problems with the national debt. But how has it affected you, and, if you have no experience in it, how can you help us, if you don't know what we're feeling?"

At last Simpson jumped in to rescue the president. "I think

she means more the recession," Simpson said. "The economic problems today the country face rather than the deficit."[28]

Simpson knew Bush pretty well and could not believe he was having such a hard time with the question. "I covered him for eight years while he was vice president," she says, "and traveled all over the world with him, and I like him personally. And I watched him and I felt . . . like, you can hit this out of the park, George. For God's sake!"[29]

I'm not sure it was such a fair question in Bush's case. Yes, he had a nice job, subsidized housing, and transportation on the tax-payers' dime. But who hired him? Nevertheless, as Simpson says, the president should not have had so much trouble answering.

"Well, listen," the president said, "you ought to be around the White House for a day and hear what I hear and see what I see and read the mail I read and touch the people that I touch from time to time." Bush described reading about struggling families and teenage pregnancies on a bulletin board while visiting a Black congregation at their church near Washington. "Everybody cares if people aren't doing well," he said. "But I don't think it's fair to say, 'You haven't had cancer, therefore you don't know what it's like.'"

Bush answered the woman from his stool, as he did almost every question. Clinton, in contrast, walked to edge of the stage. After countless talk-show appearances he knew what the woman—and the ninety million–plus viewers she represented—wanted to hear and see. "Tell me how it's affected you again," he said to the questioner earnestly. "You know people who've lost their jobs and lost their homes?"

"Well, yeah," she said. "Uh-huh."

"Well," Clinton said, "I've been governor of a small state for 12 years. I'll tell you how it's affected me. . . . I see people in my state, middle-class people—their taxes have gone up and their services have gone down while the wealthy have gotten tax cuts. . . . In my state, when people lose their jobs, there's a good chance I'll know them by their names. When a factory closes, I know the people who ran it. When the businesses go bankrupt, I know them. And I've been out here for thirteen months meeting . . . with people like you all over America, people that have lost their jobs, lost their livelihood, lost their health insurance."[30]

That show of empathy, especially after Bush's floundering, probably did more to secure Clinton's victory than any other campaign event. And it was prompted by a question that Bernie Shaw could not have asked, that I could not have asked. It would have been a cheap question on the lips of just about anyone in the media. When the public asked, however, it worked.

The Never-ending
Campaign

SIX MONTHS TO THE DAY after his inauguration, President Clinton appeared on "Larry King Live" to take calls. We broadcast that night from the White House, and as we sat waiting to go on the air, Clinton looked out the dark window of the library. He explained how frustrating it was to be locked in the mansion, behind tall gates and surrounded by Secret Service agents.

I told the president a story Jackie Gleason once told me about meeting Elvis Presley early in his career. Go out, Gleason advised the young star, go to restaurants, be a normal person. Presley's fame, however, soon made that impossible.

"I think Presley had a more isolated life than you do," I told the president.

We continued this conversation on the air. Clinton said his job

was frustrating for two reasons. First of all, his broad responsibilities meant he had to be very disciplined with his time. "But discipline means deciding things you won't do, people you won't see,
calls you won't make," he said. The second frustration was the
security. The Secret Service would prefer to keep him in a "bullet-
proof room" at all times, he said. But they had been accommodat-
ing, working out different routes that would allow him to go for
his half-hour run each day. "I really respect them. They've got a
very tough job, and I make it harder because I'm a real people
person. . . . If you don't spend some time with just ordinary
people who tell you what they think . . . you almost forget how
to listen and how to speak in the way most people live."[1]

Early in his presidency, Clinton spent a lot of time with his
constituents, in town meetings and through the interactive media.
One month into his presidency, he answered questions from
schoolchildren at the White House on a program moderated by
anchor Peter Jennings. In late May, he answered audience questions in the Rose Garden on "CBS This Morning," as Bush had
done on the same program the previous July. On our show in July
1993, he spoke with callers from four states, the Virgin Islands,
France, Denmark, and Canada. There were other programs, too,
and lots of "ordinary people." For Clinton, call-in shows and the
like were a way out of the White House, out of Washington. They
gave him a chance to break through the "bubble" of security and
staff that surrounds any president or presidential candidate.

In our White House interview, Clinton offered to come on the
show and take more calls every six months. And Vice President
Gore has been accessible, too, answering viewers' calls regularly
on NBC's "Today." When Gore came on "Larry King Live" two

weeks after Clinton's July interview, it was his third appearance on the show since the inauguration. Not that I minded all the visits. During the campaign, in a joint interview with Clinton and Gore, I had made them promise to come back.

"Would you appear again on programs like this as president and vice president?" I had asked.

Both men said "yes." Then they laughed. "I told you . . . ," Gore said to Clinton. "He's his own booker. He just booked us."[2]

Call-in shows fit in perfectly with Clinton's plans to run his White House as he had his campaign. To pass his policies, to "change" Washington, he would need to constantly cultivate public support, as a candidate would. Talk shows had worked for him during the election year. Why not use them as the nation's chief executive?

But talk radio and talk TV also hurt Clinton early in his term. The call-in circuit provided a forum for those who were angered by the new administration's proposals and actions. Irate opponents used talk radio to mount a vociferous air campaign against Clinton's plans to allow homosexuals to serve in the military. Talk shows also played a central role in "Nanny-gate," giving voice to the public outcry over attorney general nominee Zoë E. Baird's use of illegal aliens for domestic help. The administration and many in Congress had dismissed Baird's action as a minor infraction—until talk radio showed them the depth of public disapproval, especially over her failure to pay Social Security taxes for the workers. With the talk-show clamor building, Baird asked the White House to withdraw her nomination.

The number of call-in outlets on the radio has been exploding over many years, but the format is becoming a staple on cable television as well. And over the next several years there will probably be dozens more call-in shows on the air catering to all sorts of audiences. By 1996, typical cable subscribers may have access to hundreds of stations. Viewers with any interest may be able to tune into a network that caters just to them—the dog lovers' network, the bowling network, the Three Stooges network. In some ways this will be good for politicians and their media consultants because it will be easier to target niche audiences with specific messages. But, as Margaret Tutwiler puts it, "How are you going to get people to not click on a Goldie Hawn movie and click on an hour of President Clinton?"

After Bush left office, Tutwiler and Marlin Fitzwater formed a strategic communications firm in Washington that will try to answer such questions for corporate clients. But they are good questions for people in politics, too. "Does it mean that even though there are five hundred channels, people really only watch ten?" she asks. And if so, "which ten are those? . . . I think it's fascinating, but I don't know how someone's going to campaign."[3]

A conservative candidate could trumpet his or her position on family values on a religious network, for example, and his or her position on crime on the "Rescue 911" network. But with so many stations fracturing the public into smaller audiences, using old-fashioned thirty-second advertisements to reach large numbers of voters may become cost prohibitive—especially if Congress bows to public pressure and restricts campaign fund-raising or spending or both.

One way around this problem is to use the cost-efficient airtime talk shows provide, a solution Perot—always the shrewd businessman—figured out for himself in 1992. "You realize none of those fellows ever went on these one-hour talk shows until just this year," he said of his rivals during a campaign rally in Denver, Colorado. "They thought I was crazy. They finally figured out it was free. . . . We could use a little business thinking in Washington."[4]

Clinton's potential opponents in 1996 are already making good use of the alternative media. Perot appears regularly on "Larry King Live" and other shows, using talk programs to showcase his opposition to Clinton's budget plan and the North American Free Trade Agreement. He also plugs "United We Stand America," the grassroots organization that grew out of his campaign. Perot coyly demurs on questions about his presidential intentions, saying he wants to help the president and hopes to see Clinton's face on Mount Rushmore one day. But he has said he will not rule out running again, even for the Republican nomination.

On the Republican side, there is certainly no shortage of possible Clinton challengers. Dan Quayle is one obvious GOP contender, but he has laid low in the early months of Clinton's term. His potential rivals have not, and I press them for their plans whenever they come on the show—which is rather often.

As the highest-profile Republican office-holder, Senator Bob Dole of Kansas is his party's unofficial leader—and the inevitable subject of presidential speculation. The Senate minority leader has ventured into that arena before, as an unsuccessful primary candidate in 1988 and 1980, and as Gerald Ford's running mate in 1976. But with his experience as a campaigner has come age. If Dole ran and won in 1996, he would be seventy-three when he took office—more than three years older than Ronald Reagan was at his inauguration. The night after Bush's defeat, Dole told our viewers he would "probably not" run again, leaving the race "to the next generation." But "you never close your options," he said.[5]

Dole has already visited key states with early primaries, "vacationing" in New Hampshire in the summer of 1993. (On that trip, according to a *Washington Post* account, Dole ran into an acquaintance who told him her husband was away vacationing. "Oh," the senator asked wryly, "what's he running for?"[6]) Such trips are traditional for possible presidential candidates. But Dole is also an old dog who *can* learn new tricks. One night early in the Clinton administration, "Tonight" show host Jay Leno laid into the president harder than usual with joke after joke in his opening monologue. Leno seemed baffled by the pungency of his own quips and asked his cue-card holder to step forward so he could examine the jokes more closely. It was Dole.[7] Taking advantage of an unusual media outlet gave the senator a chance to display his sense of humor and combat his image as mean, old "Senator Gridlock," as some Democrats had been portraying him. He might not have played the saxophone or worn dark glasses, but it was a good start.

Other Republicans have talked about running, too. A week after Clinton's inauguration, former defense secretary Dick Cheney was on the show. Would he run? Cheney would consider it, but it was too soon to say, he told me. "I've worked for three presidents [Nixon, Ford, and Bush] and watched two others up close, and so it is an idea that has occurred to me."

Cheney won high marks for his cool and able management of the Bush Pentagon during the invasion of Panama and the Gulf War. But he may lack charisma, speaking with more measure than passion. And, as a former congressman from Wyoming, a western state with fewer electoral votes than Rhode Island, he would not start out with much of a natural base. But, as Cheney pointed out in our interview, that old-fashioned way of looking at the political map is a little archaic. "I don't think in this day and age of Larry King talk shows that geographical base is nearly as important as it once was," he said.[8] I certainly won't argue with such an astute point.

Cheney told me off-the-air during a May 1993 radio interview that he might announce his candidacy on "Larry King Live," as Perot did—if he decides to run, of course. And former housing secretary Jack Kemp has already promised our viewers that he will announce his candidacy on the show. Here we go again.

Kemp has appeared on the show often since leaving office and clearly wants to run, as he showed while enthusiastically talking about some of his ideas for modifying the tax code one night less than a month into Clinton's presidency. "You know, somebody ought to do something about that . . . ," he volunteered. "Maybe I'll have to run in '96 to do it."

"Are you going to run?" I asked.

"I may have to," he said.[9]

I'll keep twisting his arm.

Plenty of others are thinking about 1996, too, and many of our callers are ready to talk to them about their plans. But some resent what they see as premature displays of ambition. One such caller really laid into Kemp during a June 1993 appearance. "With all due respect," this caller said, "I think you're doing the country a disservice by running for president so early."

"I'm not running for president until I announce," Kemp responded, "and I haven't announced. And I told Larry I would do it on his show if . . . I choose to do it, but I haven't said that."[10]

Another member of Bush's cabinet who may seek the Republican nomination is Lynn M. Martin, the former labor secretary and Illinois congresswoman. Martin is outspoken and funny and has been one of my favorite guests over the years. But in June 1993 she sat on my side of the table and was guest host for an evening. The topic for the first half hour was the custody fight between Woody Allen and Mia Farrow. During the second half hour, she talked politics with Clinton adviser Paul Begala and Paul Gigot of the *Wall Street Journal.* So if Martin ran, and if Pat Buchanan ran again, we'd have two "Larry King Live" pinch hitters in the race. Talk about insider trading.

Some people are very uncomfortable with the "revolving door" between politics and the media. Buchanan was a White House aide to Presidents Nixon and Reagan. He has his own radio show and cohosts "Crossfire." Jesse Jackson, the former Democratic candidate, has his own show on CNN. Columnist and commentator David Gergen was an aide to Presidents Reagan and Ford. He now works in the Clinton White House, but has already said he would like to go back to the media before '96. "Meet the Press" host Tim Russert has worked for Senator Patrick Moynihan of New York and Governor Mario Cuomo. Mary Matalin, the political director in Bush's '92 campaign, now cohosts a call-in show on CNBC, the financial cable news network. Democratic strategist Bob Beckel, who helped run former vice president Walter F. Mondale's presidential campaign in 1984, is a frequent commentator and often guest hosts for me on CNN. And so on.

Some contend that this hat switching adds to Washington's reputation as one big incestuous family. The people in government and the people in the media covering it can all seem like "androg-

ynous Washington insiders," as David Broder put it in a controversial speech at the National Press Club in 1988.

> The people know what to do with politicians who displease
> them: They can always vote them out of office. They have no
> such recourse against us in the press. And if they see us as part
> of a power-wielding clique of insiders, they're going to be re-
> sentful as hell that they have no way to call us to account.[11]

Broder makes an interesting point, and I will be curious to see
if there is any backlash against this trend—especially given the
public's already jaded feelings about the media and politics. But I
do not agree with the sentiment. I think all of the people I have
just mentioned, and many others with similar résumés, bring special insight to political discussions. It's like the injured quarterback
who does color commentary during a game. They ask interesting
questions because they know what to ask. They've been there. As
Russert, one of the best questioners on television, puts it, "My
experience in government and politics is invaluable to what I'm
doing now."[12]

In addition to offering up two of my guest hosts, Martin and
Buchanan, as possible candidates, I have other ideas in mind for
"Larry King Live"'s role in the 1996 campaign. I am borrowing
one idea from Larry Sabato, a political scientist and professor of
American government at the University of Virginia. Sabato has
proposed that we use the show to conduct an "Electronic Primary," a free-form series of debates and town meetings with the
candidates and the public starting in 1995, long before the actual
voting primaries begin. In the Electronic Primary, candidates could

be paired up in creative combinations, with those who have particular differences battling it out on a single issue, or even a single
facet of a single issue. Afterward, or even the next night, we could
conduct on-air focus groups—with voters sitting in the guest seats—
to see how people were responding to the candidates and the issues.

The late Republican party chairman Lee Atwater and others
have long advocated setting aside blocks of television time, perhaps five minutes, for candidates to discuss issues at length. In the
Electronic Primary, candidates would have a full hour to discuss
and debate issues in depth with their rivals, and then come back
another night to talk about something else. It would be a welcome
break from the "process" questions—"What about this poll?" or,
"Your opponent says you're lying."—they get day in, day out on
the campaign trail. And voters would appreciate it, too. They would
know exactly where the candidates stood on every issue, every nu-
ance.

There are already divisions within the Republican party that
would make for lively exchanges in the Electronic Primary, no matter
who ran. Social issues such as abortion and gay rights are obvious
areas of discord within the GOP. Martin, for instance, is a pro-
choice Republican. That view is at odds with her party's current
platform, which opposes all abortions. But, as Martin explained
on "Larry King Live" two nights after Bush's defeat, her stand is
consistent with traditional Republican values, which emphasize
"limited government" in all spheres. The GOP must be open to
people of all beliefs and religions, she said, "or you never get a
majority . . . A political party is not a church. It isn't choosing a
pastor. It's a way of governing." [13]

Our other guest that night, evangelical broadcaster Pat Robertson, had a different way of looking at things. Robertson was a presidential candidate in 1988 and has since established the Christian Coalition, a grassroots group that has been very active in supporting Christian conservatives in state and local races. It has also become quite powerful in the Republican state party machinery, and that gives it a significant say in the presidential nominating process. Some moderate Republicans say the Robertson wing of the party already wielded too much power at their 1992 convention in Houston. Harsh criticism of homosexuals, strong stands on the abortion issue, and attacks on Hillary Rodham Clinton dominated the first days of the event, some say overpowering the president's economic message—and perhaps even costing him the election.

On the show with Martin, Robertson said that the press had overstated the far right's role in Houston and the campaign, seizing, for instance, on a few lines about homosexuals and abortion in his convention speech while ignoring the rest. "I think most political people believe this is one nation under God, and we want to keep it that way," Robertson told our viewers. But he was also careful that night not to appear extreme, avoiding abortion and similar issues when Martin or I brought them up. "I think people will respect those who know their point of view and stand by it, but I don't think we can be single-issue people," Robertson said.[14]

Social issues are unlikely to be the most significant fault line in the Republican race. The economy will almost certainly be the central issue in the primaries, and there is as little agreement within the party about how to deal with the tax and deficit issues as there is on abortion. On those matters, the Electronic Primary is already underway.

At one extreme in this debate is Kemp, a supply-side enthusiast and former New York congressman who cosponsored the Reagan tax cuts of 1981. Kemp, a self-described "progressive conservative," has said that there is too much emphasis on cutting the deficit. The only way to balance the budget, he says, is for the economy to grow. He would flatten tax rates, much as Democrat Jerry Brown proposed in the 1992 primaries. Kemp says that would stimulate economic growth, producing more revenue for the government to reduce the deficit. The difference—in Kemp's plan— would come from cutting spending, not from raising taxes, which he has said would limit growth. The American people "are overtaxed, not undertaxed . . . ," he said on our show a week after leaving office. "The only way to reduce deficits is to make this economy perform at high levels of growth, employment, and opportunity, and put a lid on spending."[15]

Cheney is in this camp, too, as he explained to our viewers the following night. "I don't think you're going to solve the deficit problem by raising taxes, as some have suggested," he said. "I think it will simply stifle economic growth, and if you don't have adequate economic growth, the deficit's going to grow even larger." Cheney also boasted about the discipline and leadership he had shown in cutting the defense budget during the Bush administration—an argument I'm sure we'll be hearing a lot of from him. But I don't think it will win him a lot of votes in states like California, where those cuts have wrecked the economy.[16]

On the other side of this debate are Republicans such as Dole, who told me the night after Bush's defeat that he was anything but a disciple of the supply-side theory. "I used to tell . . . a good news, bad news joke," he said. "The good news was a bus-load of supply siders went over [a] cliff. The bad news was there were three empty seats." Dole talks about the need to cut spending as much as anyone in Washington. But while he probably would not say so in as many words, I think he believes Kemp's idea of cutting taxes would be irresponsible at the moment. "I consider myself a conservative, but some people think conservatism is how much you want to cut taxes," Dole said. "My view is how much do you want to restrain spending and maybe cut taxes." [17] Dole's unwillingness to go along with the "no-new-taxes" line in 1988 cost him the bitter New Hampshire primary. I wonder what it would cost him or any Republican who shared his views in 1996.

The answer to that question is vitally important to the Republicans because it probably will play a large role in Perot's decision to run or not run. Reducing the deficit is issue number one for Perot and many of his supporters, and the billionaire's budget plans call for even steeper tax increases than the Clinton administration has proposed. If Perot decides to run because he does not think the Republicans are offering a credible plan for reducing the deficit—in other words, one like his—he could split the anti-Clinton vote with the GOP. Anti-tax Republicans hope it would work the other way, with one of their own winning a plurality as Perot and Clinton split the difference. Either way, it is a much more complicated race with Perot in it than it is with him on the sidelines.

Washingtonians are like this. As soon as an election is over, we're thinking about the next one. For me, the next great hurdle is more imminent than the next election. In 1993, I turn sixty. And as I considered that impending event throughout the early months of the Clinton administration, I found myself without a goal for the first time in my life. I have had great success in my career, perhaps no greater than in 1992, during the campaign. I really felt like our show contributed to the election process. But I would not be content waiting four years just to do it again.

On the other hand, I have no desire to retire. Every day I get to meet creative people—people in the arts, politics, great thinkers, experts. I love what I do, and I love doing it at CNN. You could offer me all the money in the world and put my name in the sky and I still wouldn't trade it, not for anything.

By the standards of the broadcast networks, our ratings are not very high. Even inane situation comedies frequently have larger audiences. But cable is a new frontier. It's free form, especially on an all-news network like ours. If we are making news, we can call CNN president Tom Johnson at our headquarters in Atlanta and extend the show, stay on the air for a few minutes or a half hour. That's exciting.

But what next? The answer came from former secretary of state Henry Kissinger at dinner in his New York apartment overlooking the East River. We talked about success. "Getting there was a lot more fun than being there," I said. "The hardest thing is not having any goals."

Kissinger reminded me about CNN's international reach. The news network is seen in more than 150 countries. Why not use "Larry King Live" as a forum for international politics, he said, as it had been on the domestic front during the election. Foreign leaders watch, he told me. Put them on the show. Let them take phone calls. A talk show is not bound by the stuffiness of diplomatic protocol. We could ask questions governments could not ask, bring rivals together to debate.

"You could do things that I couldn't do, that [Secretary of State] Warren Christopher can't do," Kissinger told me.

Could we? Why not. We could go to the Middle East, hold town meetings in Israel's occupied territories. We could conduct unofficial summits via satellite.

And anyone with a telephone anywhere in the world could participate. How's that for empowering?

I have no delusions. "Larry King Live" is not going to solve the world's problems. But we could promote understanding, involvement, interconnection. Ted Koppel, a friend of mine and Kissinger's, has already attempted many such events for ABC—in the Middle East, with visiting leaders, satellite hook-ups with foreign capitals, and so on. In a 1990 interview, the "Nightline" host reminded me of one of the first promotion lines penned for his show: "Bringing people together who are worlds apart." But, as Koppel also pointed out, CNN has more impact abroad than ABC, which is not seen in nearly as many countries.

"I mean . . . when I went to Baghdad back in August I was invited into a high-ranking Iraqi foreign ministry official's office . . . ," Koppel told me. "What's he doing? He's watching CNN. The whole time that we were talking to him, he wouldn't turn the set off. He might miss something."

"Does that make it tougher for you, for the other networks?" I asked. "Is it a challenge you like?"

"Well," Koppel said, "it is a challenge I like, because the fact of the matter is I think we at ABC, NBC, CBS are going to have to start competing with you folks overseas. I mean, overseas, you—all the folks here on CNN—are infinitely better known than Peter and Dan and Tom and I." [18]

In the spring of 1993, CNN's Lou Dobbs, Bernard Shaw, and

I flew halfway around the globe for "Asia Week," seven days of special reports, interviews, and news focusing on that important part of the world. In Tokyo, I conducted call-in shows with top journalists, American and Japanese, with political leaders, pop stars, businessmen, and three Hawaiian-born Sumo wrestlers and their "stable master." In Hong Kong, I interviewed Governor Christopher Patten and moderated a heated town meeting on the fate of democracy there when the Chinese assume control of the city in 1997. It was my first trip to this part of the world, and it was thrilling. I mean, trust me, you have not lived until you mispronounce the name of a three-hundred-something pound Sumo wrestler on international television. You try saying "Musashimaru" with laryngitis.

"The *R* is hard . . . ," the twenty-one-year-old champion angrily corrected me after several botched tries. "Just call me Phil." [19]

The Asia trip was one of the most fascinating and interesting weeks of my life—and I hope the first of many such adventures. Kissinger and Koppel were right, too. Everywhere we went, people knew us. "Where's Ross Perot?" one guy yelled while we were trying to shoot a street scene in Tokyo.

The people we met and talked to seemed to appreciate the chance to discuss their countries, their cultures, and their problems—just like the voters back home. And what was really amazing to me was that anyone anywhere in the world could pick up their phone and join in, from Fujisawa, Japan, to Columbus, Ohio.

This may be the real talk-show revolution. And with governments toppling, famine, ethnic strife, and civil wars making headlines around the globe, there is plenty to talk about.

So you keep calling, and I'll keep listening. After all, our future is on the line.

Notes

INTRODUCTION

1. *The Public Papers of the Presidents of the United States, Jimmy Carter, 1977, Book I, Jan. 20 to June 24* (Washington, D.C.: U.S. Government Printing Office, 1977), pp. 291–327.
2. "Larry King Live," CNN, Oct. 28, 1992.
3. Ibid., July 20, 1993.
4. Ibid.
5. Deborah Potter, correspondent, CNN, Sept. 30, 1992.
6. Federal News Service transcript, Sept. 9, 1992.

CHAPTER ONE

1. "Larry King Live," CNN, Oct. 4, 1992.
2. George F. Will, "Too Silly For Words?" *Washington Post,* Oct. 13, 1992, p. A21.
3. Ross Perot, interview with author, May 17, 1993.
4. Remarks at a Victory '92 fund-raising dinner in Detroit, Michigan, *Public Papers of the Presidents,* June 29, 1992.
5. "Larry King Live," CNN, Oct. 30, 1992.
6. Phil Donahue, interview with author, May 19, 1993.
7. "Donahue," Dec. 5, 1991.
8. Donahue, interview.
9. Ibid.
10. "Larry King Live," CNN, May 2, 1991.
11. J. Dorrance Smith, telephone interview with author, June 18, 1993.

12. James Carville, interview with author, May 25, 1993.

13. For a full account of this incident, see Doron P. Levin, *Irreconcilable Differences: Ross Perot versus General Motors* (New York: Plume Books, 1990).

14. Federal News Service transcript, Nov. 17, 1988.

15. Ibid.

16. Brian Lamb, interview with author, May 14, 1993.

17. "Larry King Live," CNN, Jan. 11, 1991.

18. Ibid., Mar. 19, 1991.

19. Ibid., Oct. 28, 1991.

20. Ibid., Feb. 20, 1992.

21. "Donahue," Mar. 24, 1992.

22. Statistics provided by MCI Communications Corp., Washington, D.C.

23. Jack Reilly, telephone interview with author, June 1, 1993.

24. Samuel K. Skinner, telephone interview with author, May 6, 1993.

25. Larry J. Sabato, *Feeding Frenzy: How Attack Journalism has Transformed American Politics* (New York: The Free Press, 1991), p. 11.

26. Federal News Service transcript, June 4, 1992.

27. Mandy Grunwald, telephone interview with author, July 1, 1993.

28. Ibid.

29. "Larry King Live," CNN, June 4, 1992.

30. Kevin Sack, "Clinton Sets Off Spark and Cuomo Fans Flame," *New York Times,* Jan. 30, 1992, p. A14.

31. Ibid.

32. "Larry King Live," CNN, July 12, 1992.

33. *Hotline,* American Political Network, June 4, 1992.

34. Ibid., Apr. 6, 1992.

35. Todd S. Purdum, "On the Sidelines: Cuomo Won't Run but Will Talk at the Drop of a Hat," *New York Times,* June 12, 1992, p. A15.

36. "This Week with David Brinkley," ABC, June 7, 1992.

37. *Hotline,* American Political Network, June 8, 1992.

38. Grunwald, interview.

39. Ibid.

40. Marlin Fitzwater, interview with author, June 10, 1993.

41. *Hotline,* American Political Network, June 12, 1992.

42. John H. Sununu, interview with author, May 5, 1993.

43. Skinner, interview.

44. Fitzwater, interview.

45. Remarks to members of the Spanish American community in Los Angeles, California, *Public Papers of the Presidents,* April 25, 1989.

46. "Larry King Live," CNN, July 22, 1992.

47. Dan Quayle, interview with author, June 3, 1993.

48. Fitzwater, interview.

49. Smith, interview.

50. "International Hour," CNN, June 15, 1992.

51. Fitzwater, interview.

52. "CBS This Morning," CBS, July 1, 1992.

53. Federal News Service transcript, Oct. 23, 1992.

54. Fitzwater, interview.

55. Margaret Tutwiler, interview with author, June 10, 1993.

56. "Larry King Live," CNN, Oct. 30, 1992.

CHAPTER TWO

1. Bureau of Labor Statistics, Washington, D.C.

2. "An American Town Meeting," CNN, Jan. 19, 1992.

3. Times Mirror Center for the People & the Press, Washington, D.C.

4. Ibid.

5. Anne Devroy, "Bush: 'All Is Not Well'; President Tempers Optimism on Economy," *Washington Post,* Oct. 5, 1992, p. A1.

6. "Larry King Live," CNN, Oct. 4, 1992.

7. Ibid., Mar. 16, 1992.

8. Ibid., June 30, 1992.

9. "Donahue," Apr. 2, 1992.

10. "Larry King Live," CNN, June 30, 1992.

11. Tim Russert, interview with author, Aug. 3, 1993.

12. John H. Sununu, interview with author, May 5, 1993.

13. Mandy Grunwald, telephone interview with author, July 1, 1993.

14. Rich Bond, interview with author, May 1993.

15. Sander Vanocur, "The President Carter Show," *Washington Post,* Mar. 13, 1977, p. G3.

16. Jeff Zucker, interview with author, May 19, 1993.

17. Larry J. Sabato, *Feeding Frenzy: How Attack Journalism has Transformed American Politics* (New York: The Free Press, 1991), pp. 58, 142.

18. Larry King with Peter Occhiogrosso, *Tell It to the King* (New York: Jove Books, 1989), pp. 84–92.

19. Thomas B. Edsall, "Clinton Throws Hat Out of Race; Arkansas Democrat Says He Won't Seek Presidential Nomination," *Washington Post,* July 15, 1987, p. A3.

20. "60 Minutes," CBS, Jan. 26, 1987.

21. "Larry King Live," CNN, Jan. 27, 1992.

22. Howard Rosenberg, "The Tabloid Tendencies of Television," *Los Angeles Times,* July 29, 1992, p. F1.

23. "Larry King Live," CNN, Jan. 27, 1992.

24. "Nightline," ABC, Jan. 27, 1992.

25. Times Mirror Center for the People & the Press, Washington, D.C.

26. Zucker, interview.

27. Ibid.

28. "Donahue," April 1, 1992.

29. Phil Donahue, interview with author, May 19, 1993.

30. James Carville, interview with author, May 25, 1993.

31. David Broder, "A New Assignment for the Press," Press-Enterprise Lecture Series, delivered at the University of California, Riverside, Feb. 12, 1991.

CHAPTER THREE

1. Larry King with Peter Occhiogrosso, *Tell It to the King* (New York: Jove Books, 1989), pp. 81–82.

2. Morris K. Udall tells a version of this tale in his collection of political humor. Morris K. Udall with Bob Neumann and Randy Udall, *Too Funny to Be President* (New York: Henry Holt and Company, 1988), p. 17.

3. "Larry King Live," CNN, July 12, 1992.

4. Mario M. Cuomo, telephone interview with author, Aug. 18, 1993.

5. Al Gore, interview with author, June 15, 1993.

6. Cuomo, interview.

7. Memorable sound bites from a 1984 debate between former vice president Walter F. Mondale and Senator Gary Hart; a debate between President Ronald Reagan and Mondale later that year; and between vice presidential nominees Lloyd Bentsen and Dan Quayle in 1988. See Mark Stencel, "Great Debate Moments," *Washington Post,* Oct. 9, 1992, p. A16, for these and other examples.

8. Richard Nixon, *In the Arena: A Memoir of Victory, Defeat, and Renewal* (New York: Simon & Schuster, 1990). p. 219.

9. Paul E. Tsongas, interview with author, May 13, 1993.

10. "Larry King Live," CNN, May 2, 1991.

11. Federal News Service transcript, Jan. 30, 1992.

12. Tsongas, interview.

13. Christopher B. Daly, "Tsongas Confirms His Abdominal Cancer, Says He Still Aspires to Presidency," *Washington Post,* Dec. 1, 1992, p. A4.

14. Mary Alma Welch, "Names & Faces," *Washington Post,* Jan. 11, 1993, p. B3.

15. Daly, "Tsongas Confirms His Abdominal Cancer."

16. *Congressional Quarterly Almanac, 199th Congress, 2nd Session, 1988* (Washington, D.C.: Congressional Quarterly, Inc., 1989), p. 102-A.

17. "Larry King Live," CNN, Oct. 24, 1992 (taped Oct. 22).

18. Ibid.

19. Kitty Dukakis with Jane Scovell, *Now You Know* (New York: Fireside, 1991), p. 19.

20. "Larry King Live," CNN, Oct. 24, 1992 (taped Oct. 22).

21. Dukakis with Scovell, p. 16. (Kitty Dukakis refers to herself in third person in this passage.)

22. "Larry King Live," CNN, June 18, 1992.

23. "CBS This Morning," CBS, June 15, 1992.

24. "Larry King Live," CNN, Oct. 5, 1992.

25. Michael K. Deaver, interview with author, May 18, 1993.

26. "Good Morning America," ABC, Oct. 30, 1992.

27. "Larry King Live," CNN, July 15, 1992.

28. Al Gore, interview with author, June 15, 1993.

29. "Larry King Live," CNN, Sept. 9, 1992.

30. Gore, interview.

31. Transcript downloaded from CompuServe, May 13, 1992.

32. "Larry King Live," CNN, Mar. 25, 1992.

33. "Nightline," ABC, April 9, 1992.

34. Robert M. Tecter, telephone interview with author, July 21, 1993.

35. "Larry King Live," CNN, Oct. 7, 1992.

36. Marlin Fitzwater, interview with author, June 10, 1993.

37. "Larry King Live," CNN, Oct. 7, 1992.

38. Dan Quayle, interview with author, June 3, 1993.

39. "Larry King Live," CNN, Oct. 27, 1992.

40. Ibid., Feb. 19, 1992.

41. Tom Rosenstiel, *Strange Bedfellows: How Television and the Presidential Candidates Changed American Politics, 1992* (New York: Hyperion, 1993), pp. 167–68.

42. Deaver, interview.

43. Federal News Service transcript, Jan. 13, 1993.

44. "Larry King Live," CNN, Jan. 10, 1991.

45. Ibid.

46. Nixon, *In the Arena,* p. 266.

CHAPTER FOUR

1. "Larry King Live," CNN, Oct. 29, 1992.

2. Ibid., Oct. 4, 1992.

3. Sharon Holman, interview with author, May 17, 1993.

4. "Larry King Live," CNN, Feb. 20, 1992.

5. "If Drafted, Perot Says He'd Run," *Los Angeles Times,* Feb. 22, 1992, p. A18.

6. Doron P. Levin, "Another Candidate? Billionaire in Texas Is Attracting Calls to Run, and $5 Donations," *New York Times,* Mar. 7, 1992, sec. 1, p. 11. Levin's book is *Irreconcilable Differences: Ross Perot versus General Motors* (New York: Plume Books, 1990).

7. Tom Rosenstiel, *Strange Bedfellows: How Television and the Presidential Candidates Changed American Politics, 1992* (New York: Hyperion, 1993), p. 164.

8. "This Week with David Brinkley," ABC, Mar. 22, 1992.

9. David Gergen, "Ross Perot's Time to Saddle on Up," *U.S. News & World Report,* Mar. 16, 1992, p. 38.

10. Ross Perot, interview with author, May 17, 1993.

11. Ibid.

12. John H. Sununu, interview with author, May 5, 1992.

13. "Today," NBC, June 11, 1992.

14. Jeff Zucker, interview with author, May 19, 1993.

15. Times Mirror Center for the People & the Press, Washington, D.C.

16. "Larry King Live," CNN, June 4, 1992.

17. Quote from June 12, 1992, excerpted on "Larry King Live," CNN, June 24, 1992.

18. "All Things Considered," NPR, May 13, 1992.

19. "Larry King Live," CNN, June 24, 1992.

20. "Who Is Ross Perot?" ABC, June 29, 1992.

21. "Today," NBC, June 11, 1992.

22. "Who Is Ross Perot?"

23. "Larry King Live," CNN, Feb. 20, 1992; see also chapter 1.

24. Ibid., June 24, 1992.

25. Federal News Service transcript, July 16, 1992.

26. "Larry King Live," CNN, July 17, 1992.

27. Ibid., Feb. 20, 1992.

28. Ibid., July 17, 1992.

29. Tom Johnson, telephone interview with author, June 25, 1993.

30. Perot, interview.

31. Ibid.

32. Edward J. Rollins, interview with author, May 18, 1993.

33. "Larry King Live," CNN, Sept. 28, 1992.

34. "Today," NBC, June 11, 1992.

35. News conference, Sept. 28, 1992, excerpted on "Larry King Live," CNN, Sept. 28, 1992.

36. "Larry King Live," CNN, Sept. 28, 1992.

37. Ibid., Oct. 27, 1992.

38. Ibid., Oct. 28, 1992 and Oct. 29, 1992.

39. Ibid., Oct. 29, 1992.

40. *Congressional Quarterly Almanac, 102nd Congress, 2nd Session, 1992* (Washington, D.C.: Congressional Quarterly, Inc., 1993), p. 101-A.

41. "Larry King Live," CNN, March 31, 1992.

42. Rollins, interview.

43. *Congressional Quarterly Almanac,* p. 135-A.

44. Perot, interview.

CHAPTER FIVE

1. Tom Shales, "On the Tube: All Talked Out," *Washington Post,* Nov. 2, 1992, p. D1.

2. "Larry King Live," CNN, May 2, 1991.

3. Dan Quayle, interview with author, June 3, 1993.

4. John H. Sununu, interview with author, May 5, 1993.

5. "Larry King Live," CNN, Oct. 30, 1992.

6. Ibid.

7. Marlin Fitzwater, interview with author, June 10, 1993.

8. "Larry King Live," CNN, June 4, 1992.

9. Ibid., July 22, 1992.

10. The Reuter Transcript Report, Mar. 19, 1993.

11. Tim Russert, interview with author, Aug. 3, 1993.

12. Phil Donahue, interview with author, May 19, 1993.

13. "Donahue," Oct. 6, 1992.

14. "CBS This Morning," CBS, July 1, 1992.

15. "Larry King Live," CNN, July 22, 1992.

16. Dan Quayle, interview with author, June 3, 1992.

17. "Larry King Live," CNN, Oct. 5, 1992.

18. "Donahue," Apr. 2, 1992.

19. Ibid., Mar. 23, 1992.

20. Michael K. Deaver, interview with author, May 18, 1993.

21. Mandy Grunwald, telephone interview with author, July 1, 1993.

22. "Larry King Live," CNN, July 17, Oct. 7, 20, and 30, 1992.

23. Richard Nixon, *In the Arena: A Memoir of Victory, Defeat, and Renewal* (New York: Simon & Schuster, 1990), p. 267.

24. "Larry King Live," CNN, Sept. 3, 1992.

25. "Today," NBC, June 9, 1992.

26. Ibid., June 11, 1992.

27. "Larry King Live," CNN, July 15, 1992.

28. Times Mirror Center for the People & the Press, Washington, D.C.

29. Deaver, interview.

30. Gary Hart, interview with author, May 12, 1993.

31. Al Gore, interview with author, June 15, 1993.

CHAPTER SIX

1. "Larry King Live," CNN, Nov. 2, 1992.

2. "Good Morning America," ABC, Oct. 30, 1992.

3. *Congressional Quarterly Almanac, 102nd Session, 1992* (Washington, D.C.: Congressional Quarterly Inc., 1993), p. 6-A.

4. Times Mirror Center for the People & the Press, Washington, D.C.

5. Mario M. Cuomo, telephone interview with author, Aug. 18, 1993.

6. Federal News Service transcript, March 18, 1992.

7. "Larry King Live," CNN, Oct. 5, 1992.

8. James Carville, interview with author, May 25, 1993.

9. "Larry King Live," CNN, July 22, 1992.

10. Carville, interview.

11. Paul E. Tsongas, interview with author, May 14, 1993.

12. Mandy Grunwald, telephone interview with author, July 1, 1993.

13. Tim Russert, interview with author, Aug. 3, 1993.

14. Gary Hart, telephone interview with author, May 12, 1993.

15. Ibid., May 17, 1993.

16. "Larry King Live," CNN, Jan. 8, 1992.

17. John H. Sununu, interview with author, May 5, 1993.

18. Ross Perot, interview with author, May 17, 1992.

19. "Today," NBC, June 11, 1992.

20. Bernard Shaw, interview with author, May 25, 1993.

21. "Donahue," April 6, 1992.

22. Phil Donahue, interview with author, May 19, 1993.

23. "Donahue," April 16, 1992.

24. Phil Donahue, "Let Bush and Clinton Meet Alone," *Washington Post,* Sept. 13, 1992, p. C4.

25. Deborah Potter, correspondent, CNN, Sept. 30, 1992.

26. Federal News Service transcript, Sept. 30, 1992.

27. Carole Simpson, interview with author, June 20, 1993.

28. *Congressional Quarterly Almanac, 102nd Congress, 2nd Session, 1992* (Washington, D.C.: Congressional Quarterly Inc., 1993), p. 117-A.

29. Simpson, interview.

30. *Congressional Quarterly Almanac.*

CHAPTER SEVEN

1. "Larry King Live," CNN, July 20, 1993.

2. Ibid., Oct. 5, 1992.

3. Margaret Tutwiler, interview with author, June 10, 1993.

4. Federal News Service transcript, Oct. 28, 1992.

5. "Larry King Live," CNN, Nov. 4, 1992.

6. Ann Devroy, "Not 'Fishing'—Just Testing the New Hampshire Waters," *Washington Post,* Aug. 20, 1992, pp. A8-9.

7. *Hotline,* American Political Network, June 4, 1993.

8. "Larry King Live," CNN, Jan. 27, 1993.

9. Ibid., Feb. 18, 1993.

10. Ibid., June 23, 1993.

11. David Broder, "Beware the 'Insider' Syndrome: Why Newsmakers and News Reporters Shouldn't Get Too Cozy," *Washington Post,* Dec. 4, 1988, "Outlook," p. 1.

12. Tim Russert, interview with author, Aug. 3, 1993.

13. "Larry King Live," CNN, Nov. 5, 1992.

14. Ibid.

15. Ibid., Jan. 26, 1993.
16. Ibid., Jan. 27, 1993.
17. Ibid., Nov. 4, 1992.
18. Ibid., Dec. 14, 1990.
19. Ibid., Mar. 29, 1993.